DAT   OR RETURN

The World Wired Up

Unscrambling the new communications puzzle

Brian Murphy

Brian Martin Murphy is Ottawa Correspondent for InterPress, a Third World news agency. He has previously worked as a writer, editor, production manager, broadcaster and computer-communications consultant in Canada, Scotland, London, South and West Africa. He is author of 'Scottish Community Newspapers', 'A broadcasting Service for Distance Education', and 'Scotland in the Multinational World' (with Alan Sinclair and Stephen Maxwell).

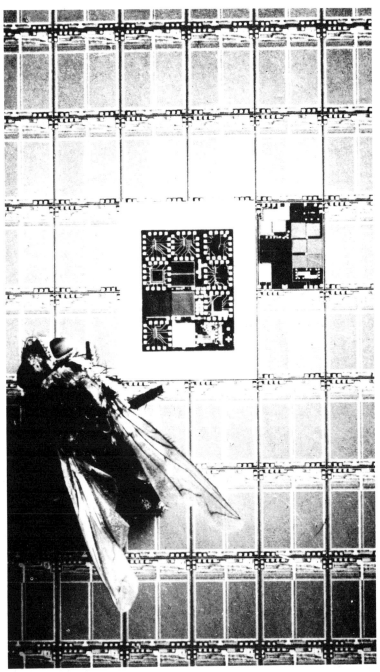

All you need to process data can be incorporated on a chip of silicon less than one-tenth the size of a postage stamp.

310697

Comedia Publishing Group
9 Poland St, London W1V 3DG Tel: 01-439 2059

Comedia Publishing Group (formerly Minority Press Group) was set up to
investigate and monitor the radical and alternative media in Britain and
abroad today. The aim of the project is to provide basic information,
investigate problem areas, and to share the experiences of those working
within the radical media and to encourage debate about its future
development.

First published in 1983 by Comedia Publishing Group, 9 Poland Street,
London W1V 3DG. Tel: 01-439 2059
We would like to thank the Educational Broadcasting Corporation and
GWETA for permission to quote from the transcript of the MacNeil-Lehrer Report.
We would like to acknowledge the financial assistance of the Broadcast-
ing Research Unit of the British Film Institute.

ISBN 0 906890 24 1 (paperback); ISBN 0 906 890 25 X (hardback)

Designed by Eve Barker
Illustrations drawn by Sandra Oakins
Photographs from The Techno/Peasant Survival Manual
Typeset by Dorchester Typesetting Group Limited, Trinity St, Dorchester
DT1 1UA
Printed in Great Britain by Unwin Brothers Limited, The Gresham Press,
Old Woking, Surrey
Trade Distribution by Marion Boyars, 18 Brewer St, London W1

Contents

Prologue

'. . . Life such as men make it out to be, a thing of sudden appearances out of nowhere, of clashes of wills and powers, of direct and violent confrontations . . . Don't think yourself as a mad and most singular man, cavalier, for it is the custom among males to find the horizon that will lead them to the absolute by playing with the lives of women . . . but it is a game played without accepting the risk, senhor, as children play with toads . . .' (*New Portuguese Letters: The Three Marias*, Paladin books, 1975).

This book is about people. Mostly it is about men already committed to the reproduction of a hierarchy in which they have a vested interest by virtue of birth. As they tell their stories, they explain a new phenomenon called 'computer-communications'.

. . . It was just after five and the operators, all women, had left for home. The men lounged around the machines, legs splayed out, some up on desks, others straddling chairs. The room was full of cigarette smoke. The fantasies ran like tap water. Each tried to outdo the other. No one was really listening to anyone but himself. Camaraderie was expressed through intonation, an inclination of the shoulders, an abrasive stream of consonants. This was a bull session.

The talk was computers – which new models were best suited to the company, where they might be positioned in the system for maximum effect. Later the rant broadened to society itself – what could happen if the telecommunications system was completely privatised; which company was best placed for a quick assault on the new market; what that market could grow to be. There was no doubt in anyone's mind that social change of dramatic proportions was on the doorstep. Our whole way of looking at life and work might have to shift. There would be new leisure opportunities. There would be more exciting jobs to do.

It could have been a gaggle of 11 year old boys crouched in an abandoned shed at the bottom of a garden. Wooden guns at the ready, each tries to out bid the other with his estimation of the danger they face, the tactics implied, the courage required, and the thrill of winning in the end. It's all terribly exciting.

. . . In the office of a New York stockbroker conversation abates while a woman delivers cups of coffee all round. She leaves and the patter starts up again. The talk is pure locker room. Sides are taken, strategies mapped out. The computer-communications revolution is charged with the electricity of a commando raid. Corporations are seen as armies facing one another across the battlefield of the stock market.

. . . In another office the 'mad genius' sits in front of his micro-computer. He waxes lyrical about potentialities, storage capabilities, information exchanges, instant reproduction. It is the stuff of revolution, immediate, incandescent. It could change the nature of human interaction, he says.

. . . The books pour forth. Authors explain the time and labour-saving characteristics of the new machines. Their image is of a woman in her kitchen.

The video terminal displays today's recipe while the computer manages cooking, cleaning and the ambient temperature. She never speaks.

. . . In the African broadcasting centre five males and two females (appointed as a result of pressure from a Western development agency) discuss the new 'non-formal' education campaign. It will use video and micro-computers to teach women in villages more efficient cooking and hygiene techniques.

Their conversation is highly technical. They talk of penetration levels, take-up rates, medium-term evaluation and long-term follow-up. The women remain silent.

. . . The Malaysian development agency brochure addresses itself to Western managers searching out micro-electronic assembly plant sites: 'The manual dexterity of the oriental female is famous the world over . . . Who, therefore, could be better qualified by nature and inheritance to contribute to the efficiency of a bench assembly production line than the oriental girl?'

. . . Japanese interactive home information experiments are conducted in afternoon hours. They reach women and children only. The male researchers are surprised to find the information is largely ignored. Nevertheless, they push on with the original concept. It was pioneered by the men at the Ministry of International Trade and Industry. It will provide the products that will bring prosperity through foreign sales. This is an important edge to have in the world economic battle. As a side effect it might change the structure of society and bring 'good things'. The experiments will continue.

. . . 'We have brought you here today to show you a major television advance which will change our lives,' says the British television executive. 'One hundred homes in the North West have been given experimental television sets which allow response to questions by pushing buttons on a hand-held calculator type channel selector. Here, if you'll look at the televisions nearest you, is the result of a recent opinion poll conducted in this way.'

In the women's toilets below the hall where this cocktail event is taking place the talk is not of a revolutionary home information service. There is a response rehearsal in progress. Voices are raised and lowered in ritual tones. Back in the hall these tones are deployed to register support for whatever the male providers plan to do. No one listens.

. . . 'For all intents and purposes we live under a male dictatorship when it comes to media. Like any other dictatorship that controls the channels of communication it can produce material that reflects its interests and promotes its image favourably. It can censor what it finds subversive. It can push its own propaganda.' (Dale Spender in notes for a talk to the Edinburgh International Television Festival, September 1982.)

There is nothing new in all this. Communications institutions reflect the structure of society, and underlining the social, political and economic definitions of that structure is the fundamental dominance of unreconstructed men. This is an important fact to remember while reading this book.

The pages that follow examine a technological configuration called computer-communications which, it is advanced, will revolutionise everyday life. Long-standing institutions are pushing this configuration on the status quo. Protests are drowned in a flood of determinist rhetoric. We are told that even if the technologies themselves do not change mankind (sic) they will at least provide new resources and outlooks. There are various political and economic arguments for and against the introduction of computer-communications. These are important problems of social management and administration. But they are all enclosed within the world of the cavalier.

The book tells the story of how the 'tools of a new era' are coming into play. This is a story, essentially, about products and markets. It is simply impossible to separate the tools from their environment. Most of the material currently available on the 'information revolution' talks about the tools alone. If this book does anything to redress the balance it will have succeeded.

There is a glossary which gives a primer in the technologies themselves. It is simple. It is not intended for those who already have some grasp of the technical innards of computers and communications machinery. It is there to provide a set of definitions for the many technologies and systems mentioned in the text.

Many of the people I have met while preparing this book have given information and shared their environments with open minds. It is not possible to name all of them. In some places the 'new communications' are a matter of consumer choice and negotiation between governments, corporations and trade unions. But there are others where aspects of the 'new age' have been appropriated by elites bent on maintaining positions of power and dominance. These sectors, in the Northern as well as the Southern hemisphere, are becoming dangerous purgatories. Sadly, information technology, which holds so much potential for assisting the development of equality, has already started to increase the efficiency and intensity of repression. To those on the receiving end it heralds an age where individuals of free mind and independent nature will be pushed to the margins. Viewing their courage in the face of implacable obstacles and hopeless odds has been a sobering and humbling experience.

No single book can change these inevitabilities. To ensure this publication does not increase the vulnerability of its correspondents, identities have therefore been masked. Some of the people in this book are real. Others are stereotypes. In most cases names and places have been re-arranged.

For the work itself, its presentation and its failures, I must bear responsibility. But there are, in addition to those mentioned above, many to whom I am indebted and can thankfully acknowledge here. These are Ian Baird, Russell Southwood and Crispin Aubrey for editing, Andy Swales and Andrew (Mintz) Illius for technical and personal assistance, Charles Landry, Dave Morley, Frances Lochtie, Ian Maxwell, Seth Sieglaub at the International Mass Media Research Centre, Paris, Kevin Robbins, Claire Coote, Paul Wilman, John Goodman, Jackie Blumler, Richard Webb, Mirchell Bier, Tom McPhail, J. Weston and the Carleton University School of Journalism, Ottawa, Jane Northey, Karen Paulsell at the New York University interactive telecommunications research unit, Christine Small, David Gallagher, Alan Marshall, Alan Sinclair, John Spencer, Gail Young, Marjory Wilson, Jack Shea, Evonne Baginski, and most particularly Lucy and Fred Murphy, whose financial and theoretical support was essential to completion of the project.

Introduction
Marketing the electronic future

Pick up virtually any magazine or newspaper these days and you will be told, by advertising or editorial, that the electronic future is here. This is a future in which the world will run on digital telecommunications networks, fibre optic cables and satellites, in which your home will become an 'interactive information/entertainment centre', your office a filling station on the 'electronic highway' – and everything from your bank account to your back-ache will be processed through a computer.

Such is the urgency with which this 'technological revolution' in communications is being pushed, by governments and private business alike, that we are told that if we don't 'cable up', 'digitalise' or get a 'bird' in the sky as soon as possible, our society will be left behind in the dust of history. The public must choose quickly, with its cash or with its vote. And once these technologies are there, we are told, there will be an increase in democracy (as more people have access to the government via interactive television), society will be better managed, resources will be more equally apportioned, and leisure time will become more fulfilling.

Cables – at the centre of this new society – will deliver more entertainment and information than ever before. Satellites, which send the signals to cables, will make long distance communication cheaper than ever before. And those who can afford it will be able to set up dish aerials and receive direct satellite broadcasts. At the other end from these new 'delivery' systems, the computer has become so sophisticated that it can mimic the human voice and conduct conversations. Miniaturisation means that micro-computers can now be added to the phone line coming into a house to provide a data network at your finger-tips.

But although all these machines undoubtedly add up to a 'revolution', there is nothing entertaining or informative about the machinery itself. A computer and its keyboard is just so much wire and metal in an attractive box. Satellites are simply hunks of transistors floating in space. These machines are tools, and tools are used for specific jobs. Yet the current debate about what will be called here 'computer-communications' does not revolve around content. It revolves around the tools in and for themselves.

In fact it is not yet clear whether the nations caught up in the rush to acquire these new tools have any clear idea themselves of *what* they will use them for. Many have not even asked whether increased information and entertainment demand is best served by satellites and cables, by using already existing technology or by changing the political and economic rules which control communications. But to say these things is to stand in the path of a hurtling bandwagon: we are being encouraged to make a choice of tools before we know what we want from them. So who is rushing this decision?

Computer-communications technologies have a lot to do with the Cold War. The United States governments of the 1950s wanted to have the slickest security-intelligence technologies, and they wanted to be the first into space. US electronics and aerospace corporations therefore received massive subsidies to develop computers, satellites and the associated technologies of the microchip, the micro-processor, digital telecommunications and the micro-computer.

These corporations used such innovations to increase their efficiency, to handle high volumes of fast computations and to maintain communication with their associates and subordinates. And with these innovations the American corporations began to outstrip all competition. With their government contracts they were cash rich, they thrived on expansion, and as they expanded they ate everything in their path and made the survivors copy their way of life to stay alive.

The 'technological revolution' *is* American, and the American people don't question these new technologies. It is enough that they are part of the American tradition of innovation for and by itself.

The conquest of social change by new technologies in the hands of a few large and hungry corporations is also seen to be the 'free market' asserting its dynamic role. Governments bow to the 'genius of the marketplace' and loosen the strings of regulation. Telecommunications and computer corporations are allowed to roam free in the economy, battling it out for control of the 'new' market for new technologies.

The American corporations – by application of their purpose-built computer-communications tools and a lot of help from the US state – have helped to create the American world economy. When these corporations shiver the world market shakes, when the corporations are allowed to sell their innovations in a 'free' market the world economy is caught up in a fever to adopt these new technologies or perish. There is no either/or about this state of affairs, the American world economy is a fact, and to mitigate its effect on their economic independence most Western industrial nations (and Japan) have tried to reach some accommodation with this all-encompassing umbrella.

Canada, closest to the Americans, created legislation to protect and encourage its own cultural and economic autonomy. Against a history of US domination of the Canadian economy and fifteen years' uncontrolled expansion in cable television (largely showing American programmes), the government decided that it must support the move into 'new technologies' if any semblance of a Canadian national component in this new market were to be sustained.

But when the government paid for Canadian communications innovations, the response from the companies was that they could only make them profitable by selling in the US market. Canadian people are in practice making the tools for someone else while their own media system is programmed to another nation's priorities. At the same time, the national agency charged with operating the legislation brought in to protect and encourage Canadian culture in the media is under fire for conducting censorship. A regulatory agency given the power only to say 'no' faces inevitable contradictions when new communications technologies appear for which there is no legislation.

European nations, meanwhile, reacted to the 'American challenge' by throwing their state budgets behind national corporations. This tactic failed. The European national markets were just not large enough to generate the funds needed to compete with the Americans, at home or abroad.

Next, the Europeans sought alliances between various corporations in the same fields. These have had mixed effects. Some governments and companies have decided to 'cede' large areas of their communications economies to American and, increasingly, Japanese corporations. But specialising in certain areas, they still hope to built up some semblance of a separate approach under the American umbrella.

To do this, however, the people of each nation must be convinced of the urgent need to take up the new computer-communications technologies. Various incentives have been tried – from the use of the EEC to develop a space programme to exchange of television programmes between nations to national schemes for viewdata networks and expansion of television systems.

The French socialist government has gone one better. Taking a leaf from the Japanese book, the Ministries of Trade and Industry have been brought together to plan the computer-communications economy. Electronics companies have been nationalised; others are being told what to produce. Altogether, the French hope their approach will carve out for the nation a special place in the 'new revolutionary era'.

But in Japan there are signs that this sort of approach has reached the end of its useful life. Immediately after the War the Japanese also formed an all-inclusive Ministry to direct industrial development, and this Ministry saw where the American electronics corporations might be vulnerable. These US corporations were placing their emphasis on large projects paid for by the United States Defense department. The Japanese decided to concentrate instead on consumer electronics, everything from stereos to calculators.

Because the government was orchestrating the financial arrangements for the Japanese firms they were not under the same 'market pressures' as the Americans. They could wait a long time to make a profit. They could invest in automated assembly lines which would not begin to pay off for years, whilst the US corporations, driven to show a profit as often as possible, moved their 'small' electronics production into the Third World – to benefit from cheap labour. When the Japanese automated factories came 'on stream', the Japanese therefore started selling products very much cheaper than the Americans, and they captured most of the world consumer electronics market. They also captured most of the market for semi-conductors – the microchips that form the basic component of all electronics products today.

At the beginning of the 1970s the Japanese saw that the future would lie in the sale of large computer systems. This was because the computer had become the centrepiece of American corporate management of the world market. Everyone wanted one for their business. Researchers also started drawing up a plan for the creation of a home market in New communications technologies, and the Ministries started planning to bring Japanese industry to the forefront of the world computer market.

Their plans were only overtaken by a downturn in the world economy. Ministries dealing with the coordinated development of the Japanese economy have less resources available; some have had their teeth pulled in political infighting. The financial structure for Japanese corporations has also changed, and they are now required to respond to a market situation, like the American corporations. Nevertheless, Japan *has* achieved second place to the United States in the computer-communications world economy by mimicking accurately the US technologies.

The Third World has had little choice about anything it experiences in the world economy, computer-communications included. The history of communications development in these nations is one in which the 'advanced' industrial nations have created the form of communications, provided the tools and the training, and then left each country to adapt. The result has been alienation, contradiction, corruption and despair. Western communications consultants return with new products and accuse the Third World of abusing the tools previously offered. It's a vicious circle – and computer-communications represent the next turn of the wheel.

Countries which might benefit more by having a useful radio system, for example, are told to drop that 'outmoded technology' and accept the latest wave of Western thinking on development. This thinking revolves around the micro-computer. Western nations with a vested interest in selling the micro-computer technology have therefore set up research centres, some staffed by scientists from the Third World, to evolve ways in which the micro can be used there. Whether, or how, it will be useful is another matter.

In Britain, the new communications technologies are taken for granted. It has already been accepted, without any well-informed public debate about cultural, educational and economic priorities, that the nation must develop a cable network, satellite broadcasting facilities and multi-purpose telecommunications systems. The debate now revolves around how, and by what form of management, these things are to be achieved.

Researchers advising the government on the 'cabling up' of Britain say the only way the system might pay for itself in the short term would be by the sale of entertainment to television viewers. But the cable companies operating an experimental service through existing cables say that entertainment services cannot hope to generate the income capable of paying for the private sector cabling of Britain. Satellite enthusiasts say the sale of programmes throughout Europe to cable companies will pay for this.

The researchers also say that the long-term benefit of having a cable system will be the introduction of multi-faceted services, including computer information services. But at least one computer information service, Prestel, has failed to find a mass market in Britain, and its operator, British Telecom, has had to re-focus the Prestel marketing pitch towards the business community. Meanwhile, British companies have already had permission to build their own cable network, Mercury. It will carry all the interactive services envisaged for the computer-communications era.

Britain has been deeply affected by the American world market. There is more US capital in Britain than in any other single European nation. American corporations have created a series of concentrations in British industry, particularly electronics. There are very few British computer-communications companies left, and those that are seem dwarfed by the US corporations. And when the American corporations introduced computer-communications technologies into Britain, they did so to serve the interests of US business and the American entertainment industry.

The present Conservative government wants to privatise the British economy, and one area where it will be easy to force this policy is in computer-communications, whose new technologies fall outside established practices. By allowing the private sector to develop computer-communications the Conservative government will provide a showplace for private industries. As part of the scheme the telecommunications utility, British Telecom, will be denationalised, largely because that private industry needs access to British Telecom lines in order to make the cabling of Britain profitable. In effect, these tools, formed to another nation's priorities, are being introduced quickly to confirm the Conservative government's hold on the economy and to develop further its alliance with the private sector.

Current Labour Party policy on these new technologies is less than helpful. It consists of 'nationalisation'. Yet the major nationalised utility, British Telecom, has proved incapable of innovation and service. It is strangling itself in its own bureaucracy. Brute nationalisation of the new technologies in communications will achieve nothing more than confirming Labour Party control of the economy.

If computer-communications are here to stay, we either have to accept the form in which these tools appear – or provide alternatives. But at present most of the thinkers and doers in the 'broad left' of politics are prepared only to say 'no'. They see the introduction of the new technologies as a conspiracy against the working people of the world. They say this conspiracy has been planned and hatched by multinational corporations. They lay emphasis on the negative aspects of the new technologies. They show how these tools are being used by oppressive capitalist organs to maximise their own profits and increase the suffering of all peoples.

Computer-communications tools are indeed doing these things. It is important that the damage be reported. But whether or not there is a conspiracy, the finding of it will not change the fact that the tools are in place and are causing new configurations of class and sexual relations.

The trade union movement in Britain and other countries has spearheaded the 'no' campaign against computer-communications. This campaign, like the campaign against robotics and office automation is doomed to failure because it will have two fatal consequences:
1. To resist the technology wholesale will only delay or divert it to another place. The longer the delay in arguing out the definition and use of these tools, the worse will be the 'bargaining' position in the future.
2. Ignoring the tools because they might not be relevant to the 'movement' in its present form leaves the stage wide open to the corporate planners. The opportunity to define what sort of information and entertainment is wanted, and how this could be achieved, will have been lost.

There are very few people thinking about alternatives. In the United States small groups of media workers have been experimenting with 'micros' in an attempt to devise programmes oriented to the information needs of minorities, the unemployed, women, children and the political ambitions of the left. They hope to construct their own data bases and information networks. They are redefining the tools, slowly and in isolation.

Other campaigners in various US communities have forced local authorities to drive hard bargains with cable companies. The ensuing contracts make sure that the new multi-channel cable systems will have a certain proportion of their time given over to 'public access'. These stations will often be starved of funds and forced to live off volunteer labour and second-hand equipment. Yet this is still an important step forward. It is one of the first signs that the commercial companies seeking cable contracts can be made to hand over some of the technological tools they control, for other uses.

In France, a long-standing alternative media movement has met the computer-communications juggernaut head on, and rejected certain tools out of hand. They have provided a manifesto for the development of representative and community media using existing television and radio facilities. They are calling for new rules, not new tools.

In the Third World significant numbers of countries have banded together since the early 1960s to research a critique of corporate systems based on computer-communications tools. They have detailed the one-way flow of news, the transfer of cultural form through broadcasting and the subversion of local cultures through advertising and 'educational' technologies. After years of fierce debate in international forums these countries managed to get the United Nations Educational, Scientific and Cultural Organisation (UNESCO) to set up a special development facility. The International Programme for Development Communications will help each Third World nation define its priorities and fit computer-communications tools to those priorities.

The Western nations do not like these developments, even though they are piecemeal and working against terrible contradictions within each Third World stage. They would rather see Third World nations accept western communications systems, including the latest style, the micro-computer. Most Third World nations will in fact have no choice but to accept them. But their vocal stance against these forms at the international meetings will at least leave the record of having sought an alternative.

By contrast, the left and women's movement in Britain, Europe and North America has much more power. It has a wealth of financial and human resources which could be turned to defining the actual information and entertainment needs of society. There are others, technologists, who might be impressed into the exciting process of reformulating the design of computer-communications tools to serve these needs. It is a process which should be going hand in hand with the search for social alternatives to the current political and economic malaise infecting the Western world.

If this does not happen, and the computer-communications 'revolution' turns out to bring 'more of the same' in terms of programming, throw more people out of work and increase oppression and disparities in society, the left will have no one to blame but itself.

Chapter 1
The United States: Global Communications Inc.

. . . The Day They Broke Up Ma Bell

Harry Nadler is a 36-year-old New York stock analyst who specialises
in utilities – and electronics. On this winter evening, in the mountains
of Vermont, he's relaxing after a day on the ski slopes in front of his
favourite network news programme, the MacNeil–Lehrer Report.
His world is about to blow open. (See background note 1.)

Announcer:
*'Funding for this programme has been provided by this station and other
Public Television Stations and by grants from Exxon Corporation, the
American Telephone & Telegraph Company and the Bell System Com-
panies.'*

Robert MacNeil:
*'Good evening. Tomorrow, the Justice Department will formally tell the
federal court that it wants to call off its seven-year anti-trust case against
AT & T in exchange for agreeing to withdraw its charge that AT & T was
guilty of monopolistic practices. Justice has accepted an historic deal,
announced on Friday. Under it, AT & T, the world's largest corporation,
has agreed to be broken up by divesting itself of 22 regional phone companies worth about 80 billion dollars. AT & T would keep its long distance
system, its manufacturing arm, Western Electric, and Bell Laboratories,
its research division. It is being described as the biggest anti-trust agreement
since 1911, when Standard Oil trust was broken up. But the deal has
raised concerns in Congress where House and Senate committees are
examining the settlement's possible impact on consumers and the rest of the
telecommunications industry.*

Tonight, with the chairman of the House sub-committee, Tim Wirth, and AT & T Chairman, Charles Brown: the effect of breaking up Ma Bell. Jim?'

Jim Lehrer:
'Well, Robin, it's the concern over what it may do to . . .'

'That's it', said Harry. He swung his swivel chair round, put down his brandy and headed towards the wall phone at the other end of the chalet. Looking across at the talking heads he punched zero. 'I thought they'd hold off at Justice till at least the end of the month to give the market a chance to recover from Christmas. Those guys are goons.' There was no reply at the other end. 'God damn, we've got a revolution on and there's not even a line to New York.'

On the television AT & T's Chairman is on the defensive about telephone charges, saying they were bound to go up even if the local companies stayed with AT & T: 'No, no, it has to do with the introduction of competition in the long distance business. If competitors move in and take parts of the long distance business there is less left for the Bell system to subsidise local rates. And under any competitive environment it's very clear that prices have to be driven toward costs.'

'Burt, Burt is that you', says Harry, shouting into a bad line. 'Burt, listen . . . wait, have you seen MacNeil–Lehrer? Yeah, yeah, later here. Hello? Oh that's better . . . Well, you know, the mountains, yeah . . . no . . ., more snow on the television . . . Look, we've got to have a meeting by noon . . . I know, too soon, well the courts are full of moles . . . it's going to be hot on the phone tomorrow, we'll have to tape a lot . . .'

Back on the box, Representative Wirth is finishing a thrust. 'Bell and its related companies have approximately 96 per cent of the long distance endeavors; that is not a competitive marketplace yet. We hope that it will be that eventually, but it's not in that situation now.'

MacNeil: 'Do you have a comment on that?'

Brown: 'Well, it is a competitive marketplace. I guess I have to agree with my friend Chairman Wirth – disagree with my friend Chairman Wirth. You know there are plenty of operatives in this – IBM, Aetna – in the form of SBS . . .'

MacNeil: 'What is SBS?'

Brown: 'Satellite Business Systems is a combination of IBM and Aetna (Insurance) and Comsat. RCA is in the business. MCI is in the business with American Express. IT & T is in the business with Sears. Exxon is in the business of terminal equipment. So, you know, it's not Mom and Pop dealing here. It's real competitive.'

Harry was shouting again. 'Yeah, yeah . . . and get the portfolios on the locals . . . yeah, right, all of them. Illinois, Diamond State, we've got to guess fast on which will get stripped and which will get a cash kiss off . . .

Oh yeah, that one they're still buying. That's important, out west in Frisco, Pacific something . . . oh shit!' Hand over phone: 'Could you turn that thing down a moment?'

Charles Brown is finally getting a chance to give his justifications: 'The primary reason we agreed to the settlement was, as Chairman Wirth has referred to here, the 1956 decree, which restricted us and was making things very difficult, and also was preventing Bell Labs and Western Electric fruits from reaching the American public. That was a major reason. Secondly, we want to clear up once and for all this cross-subsidy business. We will not own the telephone companies; they will have no opportunity – or we will have no opportunity to do any cross-subsidizing. Thirdly, we wanted to maintain, on behalf of the American workers and American competitiveness, the intercreated combination of Bell Labs and Western Electric. This, in many proposals, was becoming very difficult to maintain. There were quotas and information barriers between these organisations, and we felt this was going entirely the wrong direction, and we ought to take this major – I'd say rather traumatic – step for us to clear the air. And I think by doing this, we're concurring with a national concensus that competition ought to rule and regulation ought to only be inserted where necessary.'

After the programme Harry poured out some more brandy and settled back into his chair. He had expected this for a long time. Anyone close to the industry could see that AT&T had to do something to get at IBM and the others. But he really thought they'd hold off in the courts for a while, because of the market. The official announcement of the settlement was like a green light for Joe Public to go wild at his brokers. 'Everyone will want a piece of the real plummy subsidiaries,' Harry mused. 'This'll be the biggest thing since the Harrisburg leak.'

It was January 11, 1982, the beginning of a week's skiing holiday Nadler thought he'd have before the carnage set in. Now he'd have to fly back first thing.

It took ten years and volumes of nit-picking evidence, but the Justice Department finally nailed AT & T to the dock before a judge with no sympathy. Nadler considered the court had them 'dead to rights'. If you wanted to buy a PABX, or even a single phone, from one of Bell's competitors and hook it up to the network you found there were suddenly lots of restrictions and no excuses. You could only use touch-tone phones. If you wanted to go long distance you had to dial 12 digit numbers. Twelve digits, and they talked about a communications revolution! If you wanted to move voice-data from your own local Area Network somehow you fell to the bottom of the protocol list. It was pretty blatant.

The Federal judge on the case, Harold Greene, had spent the best part of seven years getting more and more disgusted with AT & T's posturings. He'd already told the company lawyers it was up to them to try to get out of the Houdini's box Justice had built. It was just a matter of time until he came down with a decision which would cut the company to shreds.

But you didn't scare the largest corporation in the world that easily. They'd already spent 350 million dollars on legal fees. They knew they were buying time. Yet this was cheap at the price while they were calculating which way to jump in a communications world gone crazy.

Things went beyond Bell's control after the first communications satellites were launched in 1974. Suddenly anyone could buy a few channels, set up links to microwave towers, and sell voice/data services to businesses, bypassing Bell long lines. It could have flopped, but it took off. There was a lot of money to be made, all the more if you could offer computer services in the deal and even the full array of machines to go along.

Bell itself had been restricted from entering the computer manufacturing and services field by a previous anti-trust decree of 1956. They could see now it was going to hurt. They really wanted to get into that market, and were petitioning Congress to give them the right in a new communications Act. But Congress had been gunning for AT & T. They wanted to make sure that the Act completely barred the company from offering add-on services. Something had to crack. In the end they did a deal that helped themselves: AT & T offered up the local phone companies in return for a free run at the computer-communications market.

The result was that whilst AT & T/Bell kept the still profitable long lines, some of the local companies, like New York Bell and Pacific T & T, would provide someone else with a fat cash contract. But others could sink without trace. 'I wouldn't like to own a phone in Kansas', said Harry Nadler. 'The rates will probably triple in the next 18 months.'

. . . The Night They Booked Regine's

'I suppose it was tit for tat', said the subdued Justice Department lawyer. She'd just sat through a depressing session at a New York Federal court. 'I've been here three years. Some people have actually been on it for ten. They say the transcripts run to more than 60 million pages. Now it's all for nothing.'

She was talking about the anti-trust trial at which the government had spent the best part of six years trying to prove that IBM had conspired to create its dominant position in the computer industry through unlawful monopoly practices – including underselling and buying out competition.

In the court, 71-year-old Judge David Edelstein sat disgruntled as a junior government attorney, Abbot Lipsky, threw in the towel. 'Where is Baxter?', Edelstein asked testily. 'He's responsible for this.' On the other side of the room the IBM lawyers were jubilant. They laughed and slapped each other on the back. Regine's, the exclusive New York disco, was already booked for the celebration. The court hearing was just a formality, but they wanted to be there to see the humiliation of Edelstein, a man they had tried to have removed from the case at one point for being 'personally biased against the company'.

Assistant Attorney General William Baxter was in Washington. He didn't need to be in New York. He'd already done his job, cobbling together a settlement which untied IBM from years of caution induced by looking over its shoulder at a trust-busting judge. They were free now to be as aggressive as they wanted. They would have to deal with AT & T.

'It'll be chaos', commented one computer-communications executive. 'They can go in any direction – micro-computers, cable TV, electronic publishing, computer time-sharing, international sales. It's just a matter of time. If I were at IBM or MCI I'd be shitting myself. The question we really should be asking is how a few corporations got so powerful they could push the government off the monopoly board and carve out the future for themselves.' The answer can be found well before these historic court cases involving two of America's largest companies.

Rockets and bombs: the beginning of the boom

The five years before 1960 were not good for United States' pride. America's industries and their technological advances had won the war, discovered the bomb, and set the pace of peace. But suddenly the Soviets were ahead in the race. The Navy's rockets exploded on their launching pads while the Russians actually put them straight into space. It looked very bad on television. Premier Khrushchev made big propaganda out of it.

Congress was in uproar – panic was a better word. So the money flowed, and billions were spent on electronics and space technologies to get in front again. New machines were invented to do magically fast collections and comparisons of information, just what the security services needed. A computer industry was created virtually overnight.

The Organisation of Economic Cooperation and Development has reported that in 1959, 'research and development contracts worth almost a billion dollars were allocated to computer manufacturers in the United States. This figure is comparable to the total sales figure for computers on the civil market in the same period, and it certainly exceeds considerably all support given to the computer industry in other countries.' And the money handed out for research and development rivalled aspects of the Marshal Plan. Since 1960, the electronics sector has in fact consistently gathered 60 per cent of its research and development money from government contracts, particularly from the Department of Defense.

Corporations were quickly created and consolidated around the space race. The National Aeronautics and Space Administration (NASA) had eight billion dollars a year to spend (compared with two billion now), and some of the largest firms in the world, like Hughes Aircraft, had 70 to 90 per cent of their production given over to the government. The boom lasted throughout the 1960s, and the race to the moon followed by the need to win in Vietnam, kept the corporations busy.

The list of the main beneficiaries reads like a Who's Who of the fastest growing electronics corporations in the world, from IBM to Honeywell to Westinghouse Electric. General Electric, the largest US electronics firm, increased its turnover from five to ten billion dollars between 1962 and 1972, scooping up 30 companies in the process. RCA diversified into anything from hire cars to soft drink firms. Xerox jumped its turnover from 33 million to 330 million between 1960 and 1965. Abroad, American electronics firms set up over 1,000 subsidiaries around the world in the 1960s, usually by buying out the 'locals'.

Of course government contracts can take a long time to pay off. It may look difficult to go on an expansion spree with a fist full of IOU's. But banks just love the security of a government promise. The corporations borrowed from a tiny community of financial institutions. They purchased each other and expanded overseas. After a while most of the corporations on the government contractors list were kissing cousins through shared bank directors. They sat together in the same board-rooms, went to the same business lunches – and turned up at the same political lobby meetings.

During this time 'the corporation' also reached a new level of internal development. It could be distinguished from its organisational predecessors by its three-tier structure of administration: the 'factory' level of production, sales and distribution; the 'general office' level of accounting, planning and administration (with a heavy demand for computer-communications); and the top 'management office' level where policies are decided. Often the latter is now outside a city centre, and the separation of tasks into different areas required a degree of efficient information handling hitherto unnecessary. And as the post-war corporations spread beyond the continental United States and Canada into every corner of the globe, each level of the operation became an accountant's nightmare.

The 1960s: let a thousand computers blossom

The white ranch-style house baked in its green surround. Through the front 'beau' windows a soft incoming tide lapped the beach. At the rear, french doors were flung open on a neat landscaped garden, petering out into a fifteenth hole.

John Stalker strode through the french doors. He wiped his bronzed face with the hem of his salamander golf shirt, stroked his steel grey brushcut and poured a glass of lemonade at the imitation pearl inlaid bar. 'I guess we could get in a swim before dinner,' he said. 'Benny is bringing up some steaks around seven.' His lean muscular body tensed with excitement at this prospect. Stalker is 70 and looks 50. He has the air of a man who has taken chances and won.

Stalker was a career accounting manager in 1957 when he discovered computers. He studied them in his spare time, and when his colleagues were settling in for that final run to retirement he broke loose to start a whole new career.

'My pals at work thought I was crazy', he says now. 'Business was great. Markets were exploding, particularly in our area, white goods. Everyone was getting ready for one long cocktail party on Long Island.

'They told me I'd starve in the cold on my own. But I wanted freedom. The idea of joining a big company had always stuck in my throat. The depression had forced me into it. During all those years playing social games and office politics a little voice kept telling me to get out 'cause these dinosaurs are going down. So when the computer salesman started coming round I took my chance.

'The computer boys were hunting out the accountants. We were the people who really knew the drudgery of ledgers and files full of tiny numbers. If they could sell us on their machines they were in with a lead. I looked very closely at the computers. I talked a lot with the software people. It didn't take much education to see the machines could revolutionize every company office in America. They could shift accounts, personnel files, marketing strategies and records – and just about anything else you could put on a memo.

'As soon as I got a bit of experience I quit, took all my pension funds and

set up as a computer consultant. That was in 1960. All the really big companies were already well into computers. It was the medium-sized ones, those that were growing fast on government contracts and flirting with foreign markets, who would be eager to get some computing facilities.

'What was my biggest challenge? Well, I can't say there were very many. Most companies just wanted a mainframe in the basement to do accounts.

'But there was one. This was a family company out in the boondocks that had a few machine-tool patents – which made computer companies beat a path to their door. It was real nuts and bolts stuff, screws without heads, that sort of thing. They'd been developed for the Defense Department. Now it seemed these things were essential for easy access to computer circuit boards.

'Anyway, they couldn't build factories fast enough. From a head office in the countryside they put up five factories and 15 sales offices across America. When they contacted me they were about to set up in Europe and Latin America. Problem was the family refused to leave home. They insisted I design a computer facility that could centralize administration in this little no-account town south of the Mason-Dixon line.

'I can tell you, there were some hilarious moments. We had to tell the local state phone company they could do things they'd never heard of, then help them do it. We had designers from all the big companies down there at one time or another. In the end we got a pretty good system up. The administration department, particularly personnel and accounts, could process data from all the branch plants across America, in Canada, France and Argentina. The Marketing people could call up weekly reports from some 20 salespeople all over the world. At first these were in the form of phone reports typed out by a telephonist. But as time went by it turned into data fed direct through the phone lines.

'We got the computers to produce daily and weekly updates on all phases of their business. We put the thinkers and strategists in touch with the middle-level types, the button and pen pushers in New York and all those regions. And at the top of the ladder, the idea was to put the family in touch with its minions.

'The family also wanted to be on top of all their investments. They were playing the stock market heavily and they were vulnerable to policy changes in Washington as well as market fluctuations for the computer companies. What we did was connect a computer to a group of telex services from New York, Washington, Los Angeles and London, England. Primitive by today's standards, but ahead of its time then. It proved a corporation could put its head office just about anywhere and still be efficient.

'I think the family sold out sometime in the middle 1970s. But that head office facility is still there in the middle of rural savannah country. It was really beautiful. It was my first taste of the South. I made up my mind to get down here as soon as I could. When the big guys started selling factories and firing my executive pals around 1973 I cashed in my chips and headed South. It took about two years to find this piece of land. I can thank computers for all this.'

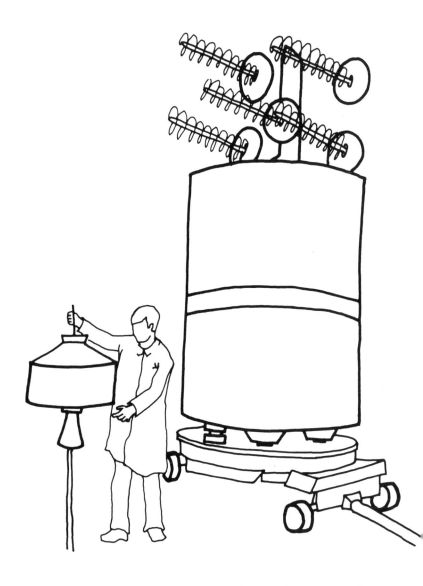

The latest satellites are much larger than their first generation counterparts. Greater rocket power has meant they can carry bigger payloads and increasing miniaturisation has enabled them to carry the circuitry for larger numbers of communications channels.

It was concerns like Stalker's Southern client, cashing in on government and electronics industry contracts, which set the pace. And the process became self-fulfilling. Government contracts brought inflated earnings and financial security which led to acquisitions and expansion, profitably executed through automation of information handling and efficient inter-sectional communications.

But as the Vietnam war came to an end and the space programme evened off, the process dramatically slowed down. By then, in the mid-1970s, banking, petro-chemical, machine-tool and electronics corporations had established more than 4,500 companies outside the United States. Each one was using computer-communications to stay in touch with head office and reduce local operating costs with efficient management and accounting, to the point of undercutting all indigenous competition.

Anyone who wanted to match up to the US corporate price structure therefore reorganised around computers, and pushed to have national telecommunications systems operate like those used by the Americans. Anyone who didn't was swallowed by the American corporations or simply went bankrupt. Meanwhile the market for computers blossomed, nearly all to the benefit of US electronics corporations. (See background note 2.)

The 1970s: the communications giants change course

Thornton Bradshaw had some explaining to do. As new president of Radio Corporation of America (RCA) he had to give his shareholders a reason why the corporation's profits had dropped 83 per cent in 1981. He blamed it on the 1970s. In a way he was right.

Up until 1972 RCA was making so much money that a finance corporation had to be purchased just to get a tax shelter. The company was top of the Pentagon's contract list for weapons systems' electronics. It was also given first choice on NASA's tracking stations, flight centres and testing ranges. That dovetailed nicely with shares purchased in the satellite company, Comsat, in 1963. RCA was definitely in on the ground floor, rubbing shoulders with AT & T, ITT and General Telephone and Electronics (GTE).

Then there was RCA's television subsidiary, the National Broadcasting Corporation (NBC). In 1965 the US corps of engineers handed over Saudi Arabian television to NBC. The Vietnam war was equally lucrative. RCA produced the radio and radar systems for all those helicopter gunships. The military satellites used RCA ground observation packages. NBC also had the contract to supply the South Vietnamese Ministry of Information with all its technical, managerial and engineering expertise. For a time NBC's international services co-ordinator actually directed operations for the South Vietnamese television network.

RCA was hit hard when government contracts fell off after 1971. Four years later, its business with the government had dropped from 33 to 10 per cent of revenues. The company blamed the 'continuing decline in expenditures by the Department of Defense and the National Aeronautics and Space Administration'.

There was another reason for its more recent troubles, however. For RCA had used its state generated cash to diversify into many companies not associated with 'high tech'. The major car rental company Hertz was one of them; and by 1980 RCA was counting on Hertz for 25 per cent of its profits. Then came the OPEC oil price rises, followed by falling used car prices and reduced demand for trucks. All these cut deeply into those profit margins. Even with 40 per cent of the market in 1981, Hertz had turned from a money spinner into a money loser. RCA resolved its crisis by selling Hertz, along with other companies like Coronet Carpets and Gibson Greeting cards, and concentrated on what Thornton Bradshaw saw as 'the future we hold in our hands – electronics and communications, particularly colour televisions and satellites'.

RCA is not alone in developing in this way. ITT also diversified widely during the boom years of seemingly endless defence contracts. Now it is reorganising to become a communications 'master contractor'. To do this, it has plans to use its Worldcom Company (leading US telex carrier with 35 per cent of the market), its electronics factories in Europe, a software research centre in Connecticut and two 'high-tech' machine manufacturers it purchased in 1978: Qume Onlot, one of the biggest manufacturers of computer printers, and Courrier, producing video display screens for IBM.

'Everyone is going this way,' says one ITT executive. 'It's the only profit sector left. Everything else is in recession. For us, diversification is no longer a simple matter of applying management efficiences to maximise returns. If that's the criteria you get into anything from bread to toys, and hope to have at least one sector on the up when others are down. It's not a prescription for fast growth, but it's safe.

'In an across-the-board recession everything is down. So you have to look for a fast growth sector. Right now it's information systems. What you want to have are interconnected interests in computer-communications with a flexible sales team going after fast growth markets. Since the US has gone for de-regulation the current fast market should be voice/data services.'

Back at RCA they've got a television network to worry about. 'It's in bad shape', says one media industry insider. 'Their ratings are so low it's an industry joke. I mean, if you've been living off the re-sale of telefilms like 'Bonanza' in 60 countries for ten years your executive producers get a little out of touch.

'RCA's commitment to the space programme through all those contracts didn't help. They insisted on hour after hour of live transmission from outer space, twice as much as the other networks, so you could see all those bits of RCA electronics clicking away. The cost was enormous. A lot of it came out of NBC's budget. There wasn't a lot left for programme planning. I'm surprised RCA doesn't sell it. But they must see some hope of linking the programme facilities up to their satellites for the pay-TV market. It's really their only hope.'

But while corporations like RCA and ITT have been reorganising round fast profit computer-communications, the very foundations of that industry are shifting. 'If I wanted to know the shape of the information age, I'd wait to see where AT & T and IBM move', says Harry Nadler. 'The government has put down its chips and left the room. The rest of the players are scrambling to reorganise while they look over their shoulders to see which game is called by the two dealers at either end of the table.' (See background note 3.)

Heads Down For the Micro Revolution

Dick was stoned. Last night he'd fallen asleep in the office at four a.m. with his cigarette alight. Only the night watchman saved a catastrophe. Later that day someone dropped by with some grass. He'd sleep now.

He hunched over the butt-marked kitchen table. 'If only I can get this system up and running we just might save the business', he mused. 'We've been running a deficit but I think I've got a programme which will process the accounts so there's something positive to show the bank. With more money from the bank I can get on to more business services. Information, that's the new resource.' Dick's dream is his addiction to his 'micro'. He really believes that this machine will solve his financial problems – and all his waking hours are devoted to working out his own specific system, by-passing off-the-shelf small business programmes from the manufacturers.

Dick Trainer is a systems worker at a medium-sized printing outfit near Buffalo. Times are hard for printers. Their regular customers keep asking for more credit, cash flow is drying up and to bridge the gap they've gone in for fast copying services. A couple of copying machines were bought on hire purchase. Then one day when the copy engineer was round he showed Dick their new line of micro-computers. He took away the brochures. It looked like magic. He could do just about anything with the machine: the accounts and billing, cash flow projections, even link up to computing services and business information offered on a group of networks he could dial up on his phone.

The price seemed right as well. The company could use the same sort of hire purchase and service schemes now familiar through the copy machines. And, as the engineer said: 'On a cost per computation basis the smallest computers today are cheaper than the largest.' Like millions of others in the United States Dick took the plunge and got hooked. With his programming manual he now sits mesmerized for hours trying to construct the systems which will pull the company out of the red.

Dick's company is part of a new market which is changing the face of the computer communications industry. Since 1975, the slice of the computer market held by large 'mainframe' makers has dropped by more than a half, but overall sales revenues have almost tripled. The boom has come in small business computers, mini-computers and micro-computers.

New manufacturers have also emerged to develop this market. They used the sales tactics of office machine makers, and left the 'mainframe'

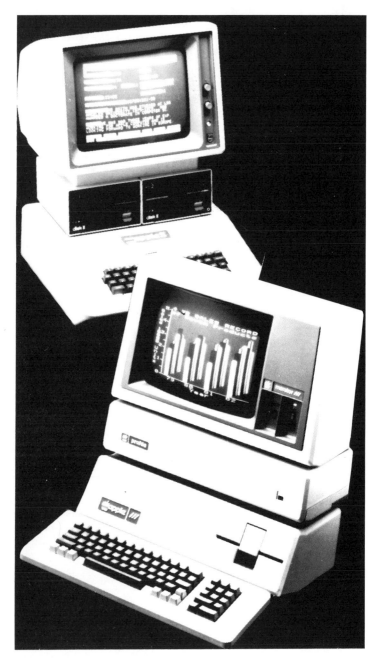

That most typical of micro-computers, the Apple. Shown here are the Apple II and Apple III. The screen on the right shows the sort of simple graphics the micro-computer can generate.

builders behind. Now the larger manufacturers are scrambling to get a piece of the action, led by IBM.

The sales approach is geared to two different levels of business. Medium-sized companies are told that their white collar workers should be served by 'work stations'. These stations are VDU's and keyboards which link up to a central computer, to a PABX (office telephone exchange) and out to the information networks. Small businesses are sold mini- or micro-computers with simple programmes and a promise of 'peripherals' to add as they can afford. They also get the information networks at their finger tips.

Both IBM and AT & T are therefore forming their short-term strategies around these markets. AT & T wants to start selling 'dedicated application' machines for attachment to their PABX systems, and to bump up usage of their proposed computer services network. IBM is selling a 'new generation' of office equipment to hook up to their own Local Area and Value Added Networks (see Glossary), and delivered through Satellite Business Systems.

And as more offices go over to computer machinery the big winners are the networks, particularly as all those companies push data (information) between head office and their branches. There are more than 500 data transmission services available in the United States today, and the two largest – Tymnet and Uninet – expected their sales to reach the 1 billion dollar mark by the end of 1982. The three main carriers for these networks are Satellite Business Systems, Western Union and RCA. Industry analysts predicted these three would also jump their sales by 50 per cent in 1982 to 660 million dollars (see Note on Satellite Owning Corporations, P. 36). AT & T itself is aiming to carve out a 100 million dollar piece of this market after 1982, with its own ACS.

'This micro-computer revolution has barely begun,' as one computer-communications executive explained. 'The medium-sized office and small business is a purely short-term market. It will reach saturation by 1990. Long-term bets are on the race to offer a fool-proof information service to the average consumer. The data networks are already in place, the short-term market will allow them to get the bugs out, and now it all depends on the cables and developing a micro-computer as reliable as the television.'

So the personal computer is at a watershed. Until 1981 they were being sold at a brisk pace specifically to people after special services and willing to learn how to make a computer work. But the big names in the field – Apple, Tandy, Commodore, as well as IBM and Xerox – are about to do things to the micro that make it as easy to operate as a telephone.

'It's not far away,' commented a salesman at a New York personal computer showroom. 'Apple and Xerox are developing machines that tell the user what to do almost from the moment they plug it in. It's called 'user friendly' and it means they tell you how to programme them, how to operate the programmes and where to get the milk for the coffee.

'The Japanese are going the "plug compatible" route. These are machines which will be capable of taking on-board programming from, say, IMB for half the price and a tenth the bother. In other words, their machine will do everything an IBM machine does, even use its programmes. But the prize will go to the bunch of companies which get to the market first with "emulators". These will be constructed with a standardised processing chip – it looks like AT & T's Western Electric have the lead for that item – and a group of chips which allow anyone's programmes to be fed through even if they're designed for other makes of micro – it'll join up any kind of machine.

'When you've got that, the machine doesn't matter so much as the software you can put through it. People are buying micros here now which will be out of date in three years. If you've got the time, I'd say wait until they are producing emulators the size of television sets with a twelve-month guarantee and no need of a service contract. Then you can sit back and wait to see who is going to win that battle of the last mile. You'll be in the driver's seat no matter which network wins out.'

The 'last mile' is a euphemism. It's mentioned a lot these days in government, computer and communications circles. It refers to the final stretch of cable between all these services and the homes of America. Whoever owns that cable will be sitting on a gold mine. With deregulation now in full flood, most regulation agencies will join the public and sit back to watch the scrap between the telephone companies and the cable TV companies.

If the past two decades are anything to go by, this battle will be a ruthless affair. Cable television is the black sheep of the US media, and for years it flitted on the communications fringe. The corporations who own the vast monopoly networks of subscribers have also emerged with a reputation for piracy and corruption. And until recently very few US televisions were hooked up to a coaxial cable. As late as 1978, only 13 million people were subscribers. But by 1983 density of service should reach half of all televisions owned, and in 1990 half of all Americans will have access to cable television.

Fleecing the black sheep

Strangely, it all started with 'Mom and Pop'-style local companies, sometimes run by the local television show room, providing cables for people who couldn't receive TV transmissions on an aerial for one reason or another. The average size of a system seldom went beyond 1,000 subscribers. That changed around 1960. Entrepreneurs took a look at the burgeoning suburbs and thought they could sell a cable link to new home owners with a promise of TV stations from distant places. The first breakthrough came in San Diego: a cable system got a licence from the city council to wire up 160,000 homes to receive Los Angeles television. Close behind came cable compan8es in New York.

Local TV stations didn't like this turn of events. There were no regulations governing the operation of a cable franchise. Operators could show anything, and distant stations started selling advertising on the basis of the new audiences reached by cable. That cut into local station advertising budgets.

Programme networks and producers thought the whole thing was a bit dirty. The cable people just stuck up an aerial and replayed programmes without paying anybody. Cable companies scoffed at the idea of royalties. The broadcasting lobby went into operation in Washington. At first the regulator, the Federal Communications Commission (FCC), refused to regulate. They said that cable fell outside the definition of broadcasting laid down in the 1934 Communications Act.

But the FCC did have power to regulate the use of microwave transmitters. The cable stations used them to transfer TV signals from region
to region. At the beginning of the 1960s the FCC therefore, told cable
companies to carry local stations only, and to drop any distant programmes which duplicated local fare. Later, in 1965, the cable companies were restricted from operating in the 100 largest advertising
markets in the country. After 1972 they were not allowed to broadcast
films less than three years old or sporting events carried regularly on
broadcast television. Further, they had to offer 'free access' channels to
public authorities when they did a deal with them on 'cabling-up' an
area.

Usually the cable operators offered a much better sweetener than just
free access – money changed hands, a lot of it illegal. Even with entry
costs made high by regulation, cabling-up an area was a once only fixed-
cast piece of investment, and those rental fees still came rolling in every
month. It was easy money. The competing companies wanted new cable
franchises so badly you could almost smell it.

From the outset it was understood that a cable franchise had to be, de
facto, a local monopoly in order to reach effective cost service ratios. It
was left to local authorities to regulate these monopolies. Each council
drew up its own rules, and councillors became the target of 'persuasion'
by the cable operators. In 1971, Irving Kahn, president of the country's
largest cable chain, Teleprompter, went to jail for giving a 5,000 dollar
bribe to a local official in a Pennsylvania town. But this was seen as only
the tip of an iceberg in which countless smaller fish turned palms green
every day across America. Companies also came up with what were
euphemistically called a 'gift to the community'. One Massachusett's
town got a new public library, another in Illinois received an interest free
loan on a new water system.

But although on the legal side the broadcasters might have had
Washington on their side, the cable companies had the courts going for
them. In 1965 a Supreme Court ruling freed cable companies from copyright liability. It left a bitter taste between television and cable. A decade
later another Supreme Court ruling threw out most of the FCC regulations. The judgement said the FCC had no right to tell cable companies
what they might show. Local wires could carry anything from movies to
information services. In the same year, Time Inc. announced it was
renting satellite channels to beam movies to cable-receiving dishes
around the country. It would be called Home Box Office, and subscribers would pay an additional fee for the channel. This was the beginning
of pay-TV, and it blew the cable scene wide open because suddenly all
the local cable networks could be linked together through satellite
networks. The large media companies began to see almost limitless
potential.

When, in 1978, Time bought the second largest multiple-system
owner, inheriting more than a million subscribers, competition to cable-
up cities became fierce. Companies fought extensive battles using the
courts, advertising and political lobbyists to win local cable TV franchises. 250,000 dollars was not an uncommon campaign budget. In one
city, Dallas, the monopoly was given to Warner Amex (a company
formed by Warner Communications and American Express). Not willing
to call it a day, the loser, Sammons Communications, went to court and
gained an injunction forcing a local referendum. After a massive advertis-

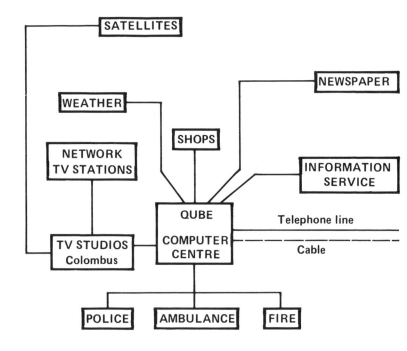

The American cable TV network Qube.

ing campaign, Warner won the ballot. The city of Boston demanded a 100 channel system with 20 two-way links for public use. The New York Times snapped up 55 local systems in New Jersey for 83 million dollars.

The next stage is the actual cabling-up of the nation's major cities, and the corporations are planning to spend heavily. Warner Amex will shell out more than 100 million dollars to cable-up 400,000 homes in Dallas, the same again to connect 300,000 televisions in Cincinnati and 48 million for 170,000 in Pittsburgh. But by far the most noticeable change in cable systems since 1975 has occurred through merger and acquisition. 'Mom and Pop'-style companies no longer exist. Ownership in the industry is also being consolidated among the media conglomerates. Cross-ownership is the trend. (See background note 4.)

'They're covering their bets', commented one Boston media analyst. 'No media company wants to get caught in the marginalised advertising medium five or ten years down the road. It was the notorious Irving Kahn who predicted that cable TV would become the information utility of the 21st century. As soon as the whole country is cabled with interactive capabilities, the home will be able to use the television for everything from shopping, banking and messaging to data retrieval, computer tasks, and home environment management. The interactive home may be some way in the future but the rush is on now, no matter what the cost, to achieve a position of de facto public utility service – because the phone companies are very close behind.' (See box describing 'Qube'.)

AT & T, for example, has never thought that cable television deserved to be a public service. Throughout the years phone companies have refused access to their wire-carrying poles, charged exorbitant rates for attachment, demanded eventual ownership of cables and declined outright to install small systems, especially in urban areas. Cable companies fought back to get the right to attach their cables to AT & T poles. But the cost was still high. Now AT & T itself is free to get into the interactive communications business. The corporation may not have direct control over local companies any more; but it does have the technologies and it still owns the phone equipment attached to the local systems.

Qube is the only fully 'interactive' (two-way) cable television system operating in the United States today. It was set up as an experiment by Warner Amex in 1977 and serves 50,000 subscribers in and near the city of Columbus, Ohio. It offers 30 TV channels, ten of them 'interactive', for which the subscriber pays extra.

The interactive label means that the viewer, holding a box like a pocket calculator, can vote in response to questions presented on the screen or take part in various styles of programme such as quiz shows. Programmes may be accepted or rejected on a one-at-a-time basis, with the computer making the appropriate note on a running account.

Banks are keen on Qube. They have been preparing to launch themselves into the interactive marketplace for some time, with the development of electronic cash machines and inter-bank computer currency exchange networks. Qube has in fact been attached to a local bank in Columbus for a while. The subscriber can call up a bank statement and conduct financial affairs through the television. Mail order houses are also keen on this aspect. The system is designed to handle transactions through credit card numbers. This is a major reason for American Express funding the experiment. The system can also offer fire/medical/ burglar alarm services.

'Because the subscriber has his own identification number and a computer sweeps his home every six seconds (for the rental monitoring service), the service can accumulate vast amounts of information on what the customers are watching, how they are voting and what they are buying. Warner officials disclaim any intention to maintain records on individual viewing or buying habits. But they acknowledge that concern about privacy is genuine, and that the potential for abuses cannot be taken lightly.' (Efrem Sigel in *Videotext*, Harmony Books, New York 1980.)

Warner Amex has signalled its intention to install Qube-type systems in all new franchise areas it obtains. The company is the fastest growing multi-system operator.

In addition to its plans for a data network (ACS), the American giant has chosen the Canadian viewdata system, Telidon, as its technical standard for a future completely interactive information network. To the dismay of newspaper publishers, for instance, the Yellow Pages will be marketed through these proposed information networks. The concept is simple enough. You go down to the local telephone shop, buy a keyboard and a modem to connect to the telephone lines, and your television turns into a micro-computer with access to all existing data, information, banking and consumer services. Who needs cable TV?

It's hardly surprising, therefore, that the cable operators have an abiding hatred for AT & T. And as the media conglomerates rush to stake their claim to a piece of cable TV, they're counting on making new alliances with hardware and software industries – particularly banking, publishing and electronics – to outmanoeuvre the giant.

For the moment no-one is making any money from cable. But then nobody thought they'd make a fortune from electric power when the first light bulb went on sale. The multiple systems owners are upping the ante for the right to control local audiences while Pay-TV companies are running big deficits competing for the entertainment side of cable – which many hope will be the hook that keeps the customer wanting more until interactive systems are in place. The only people smiling are the local operators who made the big investment in cabling-up a few years ago. They've got people beating a path to their door, spending anything to get on to that last mile. (See box on satellite TV and background note 5.)

Satellite TV – pictures from a dish

'Well, you'd be surprised how cheap this whole business will be', said Irv Spring. He was standing in front of a large sliding door which led into an old farm equipment garage. Today it was his makeshift satellite dish aerial showroom. He's been selling them for three years to people who drive into town from their mid-west farms and take them away in pick-up trucks.

The most popular is 12 foot in diameter and it's got an azimuth/elevation mount. That won't mean much to you, but it'll let you focus the dish on whichever of our 18 broadcast satellites you want to look at. I can do you one for about 3,000 dollars. But if ya want to wait a few months I'm getting in some Jap models – do the same thing for half the price.'

Irv has been on to a good number. There are 40,000 dishes floating around the US. The market leader, National Microwave, is selling 1,000 a month. Most of them are being sold out West where the cable services are trash and there are few tall buildings stopping the viewer from drawing a bead on the birds.

Owners have their own jargon. The dish aerials are called TVROs. 'That's Television-Receive-Only earth stations to you', smiled the SPACE press officer in Washington. 'And SPACE is the Society for Private and Commercial Earth Stations. We've been campaigning hard here to get Congress aware of the fact that everyone has a right to capture what's in the air. It's up to the Pay-TV companies to protect their product with scramblers if they don't want it picked out of the sky. If they're stingy and don't want to do that we shouldn't have to go along with them by writing our Communications Act to suit their needs.' The Pay-TV network companies don't like the idea that someone with a dish in Wyoming can watch their programmes for free while cable operators in New York are paying three or four bucks a head to pipe them along cables.

'Again, its their problem not the aerial owner's, says the SPACE spokesperson. 'We tell all our members to write to the cable networks and offer to pay. But their accounting procedures, all computerised I might add, don't allow for processing mass retail subscriptions. They're moaning about copyright, talking about court cases. I'll believe all that when I see it, I mean, who's going to take a hundred thousand Americans to court. They're just trying to protect their lucrative cable market.

'If Congress bans TVROs in the Communications Act there will be hell to pay. We've got a whole industry now making these things. It would be a blow against free enterprise. I really don't think they would do it.' At the 1981 Las Vegas Consumer Electronics show there were 60 companies showing off TVROs.

'It's definitely here to stay', drawled one Texas-based TVRO salesman. 'I'm selling everything I can get my hands on. You better believe people will fight hard to protect their right to watch whatever they want. For a single family it's not cheap. Now I know there are some unscrupulous fellas trying to sell some of the programmes, in bars or even in their homes, but in this kinda country word gets around and the law would be on them fast. I'm all for that. But when it comes to individual rights, well that's where I'd have to look the other way. Now, you know, they had prohibition here in the Twenties, ya heard of that? Well I see it just like that. Even if they pass a law against it, it will go on and sooner or later they'll have to make it legal.'

Up North, Ernest Hovland put it another way as he browsed through a New York TVRO store. 'It's a modish thing to do. It's like buying a boat. It's recreational, only you can use it year-round without ever having to leave your house.' Back in Washington SPACE has got another solution. 'We've offered the Pay Network people a royalty system. We, or some neutral agency, could collect it and it would be distributed to the companies. Now I think that's fair.'

Back in his New York office, Harry Nadler was enjoying the joke. 'It's almost poetic justice. These three monsters – AT & T, IBM and Cable TV – have been in and out of court for decades. Everyone is calling everyone else a crook. They all use their pull in Washington and their best lawyers in the courts, and after all the dust has settled the powers that be simply pull the walls down and let them at each other. Well, I've got to say it, it's the American way. When in doubt revert to form. In this country the customer is always right and the market sorts the weak from the strong.

'I mean what else could they do? We've got a bunch of diplomats wandering around the world talking about the need to preserve a free flow of information. Governments all over the place are trying to control the flow of data and entertainment into their own systems, and we say to do that is a blow against freedom. We'd look like real hypocrites if we turned around and started telling the computer-communications companies how to run their business here.

'No, I'm all for deregulation. It'll be good for business, good for invest-ment, good for the American economic system. But let's make no mistake, we're talking about competition between the big boys only. This is the corporate world. The government acknowledged that a long time ago. They're in the driver's seat and anyone who gets in the way will just be run over.'

The American way: recession and the public service option

The computer systems researcher raised her voice to compete with the New York traffic. 'What we're dealing with is a virtual fait accompli,' she said. 'American consumers are giddy with computers and cables, and the corporations are using these systems to drive a coach and horses through traditional industrial practices, without consultation in most cases.

'The result is that factories get computerized and have robots installed. Most of them are just closed and transferred to the Southern states or the Third World. Either way the unions, used to bargaining their way to higher wages, are left flat-footed without a proper view of what is happening around them. Their reaction, for the most part, has been to go along with the corporations on "productivity deals".

'America is hurting and the government doesn't seem to have any idea how to deal with it. Ronald Reagan's policy has been to free the market from state control to let business solve the problems of the economy. He has tried to cut back on social services while offering tax incentives for industry. It's not working, I think we should remember that. Most of the technological innovations, particularly in the communications field, have been introduced into an American economy which was buoyant – until today. This is not a buoyant economy. It's the worst it's been in 40 years, since the Depression, and no matter what the President says, all the figures point to it going farther down.'

The human statistics bear her out. Industry is working at only 70 per cent of capacity. White collar workers – the grist for the information revolution – are running an unemployment rate of five per cent. At the same time, the Federal government has restricted payments to local governments, and left them to raise their own funds. The infrastructure is starting to rot. Bridges, highways and water systems are depleted to the point of danger while construction slows to a trickle.

'I'm ready to believe that industrial capitalism has just about run its course,' says the Network researcher. 'Steel and automobiles, the pacers of our industrial development, are leading the drop into depression. If we can take that as a sign then, yes, we are at a historic cross roads.

'But we also have to remember that each dislocation in the process of capitalist development has been the signal for consolidation of monopolies around new markets which thrive through degradation of labour. I think we're seeing that. I think AT & T and IBM are the leaders of a new industrial era. They have been given the nod by the government to begin that process of consolidation. That doesn't sound to me like a revolution which will reach into the homes of America. I doubt whether the millions of unemployed, the 15 per cent of the population living under the poverty line, the millions of black men and women without jobs or proper homes and the others – millions of marginals travelling from one part of the country to the other looking for work – will be able to afford the 30 to 50 dollars a month required to get wired into the information revolution.

'That's why we're working on this project here in New York. We're looking at the capabilities of Apple and Tandy computers. The companies are paying the centre to do the work. We analyse their programmable capabilities. Later I try to use them to set up community information systems. In some small way, owned as a community resource, the micro has potential to assist people in their fight-back for survival. Right now we're doing programmes to help people get better services from state agencies, check out housing options, connect women and minorities with organisations working on their behalf, even video libraries for street schools and art labs.

'If we put this growing resource together with the free access we've dragged out of cable television systems there is the glimmer of an alternative network. I suppose the idea would be to put our own information and experience on the data networks to share with other groups across the country. It's not much, there are very few groups thinking this way, but it is one way to turn the corporate lining inside out.'

The corporations are well aware of the 'community service' option. A good deal of the research into alternative applications of computer-communications has been sponsored by the corporate research centres. The left naturally remains suspicious of these studies. (See box on Community Communications.)

Community Communications brought to you by the Corporations

Corporate research centres like funding public media. It fits in well with their commitment to the spread of American educational media techniques and programming at home and in the Third World. It also creates a high-profile 'non-profit' venue for corporate advertising.

In the United States the national non-commercial television network is called the Public Broadcasting System (PBS). It has existed for years with a small grant from the Federal government, local grants and a large subscription from viewers. Since Ronald Reagan came to the Presidency the organisation has been under pressure to integrate corporations more thoroughly into its sponsorship structure (as Federal funding is reduced). In July 1982 the organisation had to lay off 24 people, 15 per cent of its workforce.

In the meantime, corporate research centres have been sponsoring studies of cable television and Pay-TV networks to see how they might be spun off into the 'community' sector. The research has depended heavily on grants from Ford, Rockefeller and other similar, large corporate entities. One typical proposal has been funded by the Carnegie Foundation. It is called PACE. It would be a cable service for the performing arts, culture and entertainment. Here is an outline of the proposals:

'The proposed new national pay cable service for the Performing Arts, Culture, and Entertainment – PACE, for short – is one for which we believe there is a consumer need, a financial market, and, most importantly, a social value.

In the development of the proposal for the PACE Network, we sought to achieve the following objectives:

● to identify a use of nonbroadcast technologies that could be self-sustaining and still within the broad educational and cultural mission of public broadcasting;

● to structure a nonbroadcast service that improves the chances of survival and success for the primary broadcast service;

● to find a new source of funding for the support of programming;

● to enable public television to use more of its own discretionary funds on those programs that are more difficult to finance through subscriber payment;

● to devise a financial and organizational structure capable of withstanding the rigors of the marketplace, while maintaining the integrity of public television's noncommercial mission; and

● to expand the opportunities for American artists, producers, and other professionals in the expanding communications industry.

PACE will be a major bridge for public broadcasting into the new technology of the future. It will be an independent part of the public broadcasting family. It will be separately financed by a mix of public and private funders initially, and ultimately by its own audience, but as a quasi-public entity its creative decisions will always be anchored in quality, not profit. We see it as a major source of co-production with stations and independents.'

(From 'Keeping PACE with new Television', The Carnegie Corporation of New York, 1980.)

'It's difficult to find a concensus between the academics of the left, the researchers at the corporate centres and those actually working on some sort of alternative computer-communications project,' says a woman who works with a cable network in Connecticut. 'I suppose if there is one it's that cable television, with its public access channels, should be used to teach people how to use the new machinery, how to use the machinery to develop self-help structures and how to put it all together to bring political pressure on whichever institutions remain intact and capable of blunting the worst effects of this new corporate age. That's a tall order.

'On the political side the Federal authorities have more or less caved in. It remains to be seen what state regulatory bodies do with the newly independent phone companies. At the local level there is still a chance to make inroads into cable monopolies.

'Boston has set a good example. The city handed over control of a number of public access channels to a non-profit community corporation. In that sense you could say there are bourgeoning alternative networks here. But don't raise your hopes. We saw what happened to the alternative press created with the proliferation of cheap printing processes. There was that initial burst of radicalism fuelled on the Vietnam war. In some places it redefined notions of community development. It also gave meaning to the term hip capitalist.'

Background notes

Satellite Owning Corporations

AMERICAN SATELLITE
Owned by Continental Telephone and Fairchild Industries. Owns 20 per cent of Westar Satellite System. Sells voice, image and data communications via satellite.

COMMUNICATIONS SATELLITE CORPORATION (COMSAT)
Owned half by public share, half by 163 companies in the communications industry. Of the private shares, AT & T has 29 per cent, IT & T, GTE (General Telephone and Electronics – see below) and RCA each have 16.4 per cent. Holds monopoly of US international satellite communications. Has contract to manage Intelsat group of satellites (six so far) and holds 23 per cent of that consortium, to which it is sole US representative. 1980 turnover: 300 million dollars.

RADIO CORPORATION OF AMERICA (RCA)
Private share owned corporation. Diversified manufacturer of electronics and communications systems. Owns Americom Satellite system (three satellites in space). Sells satellite channels and international voice and telex services. 1980 turnover: 250 million dollars.

SATELLITE BUSINESS SYSTEMS (SBS)
Owned by IBM, Aetna Insurance and Comsat. Sells satellite channels to voice/data networks (two satellites in space, one planned for 1983). 25 corporations have built their own internal voice/data systems around SBS, including General Motors, Boeing and General Electric.

Background note 1
The new networks facing AT & T

For most of this century the American Telephone and Telegraph Company and the Bell system of phone companies have together had a de facto monopoly of telecommunications services. This is no longer the case. Satellites and micro-chips changed the state of play.

Cheap micro-chip-based telecommunications equipment allowed other companies to enter the communications market place. They sold telephones, switchboards, switching systems and PABX systems graduating to Local Area Network. But these new competitors had to fight hard against the AT & T monopoly. They used Congress and the courts to force AT & T to allow their machinery to be connected to the telecommunications networks.

From 1975 a group of companies also started using satellites linked to microwave transmitters in order to offer long distance services independently from AT & T. Most of these services transmit data only, and the signals still had to be switched through local phone networks. When AT & T agreed to divest itself of these local companies they were, in effect, freeing competitors from the constraints the Bell system had been placing on non-Bell originated communications.

With the way cleared for 'equal connection at the local level' the new telecommunications networks are forging ahead with plans to extend their reach. There are currently ten domestic communications satellites operating over the United States, with a combined total of 160 transponders. One third of this capacity is used for video distribution – mainly Pay-TV programmes – to the more than 4,000 cable TV systems. The remainder is taken up with telephone, telex and some data transmission. In addition, Comsat (see below) rents 10,000 voice channels from Intelsat for international telephone lines.

This long distance satellite system is bursting at the seams. There are predictions for 26 domestic satellites carrying a total of 500 transponders by 1985. Telephone traffic alone is expected to grow by a factor of 1.5 by that year.

Some of these services are run by AT & T. Here are the competitors:

GENERAL TELEPHONE AND ELECTRONICS (GTE)
Public company. Owns largest independent (non AT & T) telephone system in US. Manufactures telecommunications equipment and operates data communications network through leased channels. Will launch three communications satellites towards end of 1980s. 1980 turnover: 10 billion dollars.

SOUTHERN PACIFIC COMMUNICATIONS CORPORATION (SPCC)
Owned by Southern Pacific group of companies (railways, freight transport, pipelines). Operates long distance voice network. Will launch two satellites in 1984 to deliver Pay-TV programming to cable stations, teleconferencing and other video services. 1980 turnover: 152 million dollars.

WESTERN UNION
Private share company. Largest telex operator in the United States. Has two satellites (Westar), with more planned. Operates telex, telegraph and other data services via satellites. Rents satellite channels. Recently allowed to compete for international communications destinations from the United States. 1980 turnover: 794 million dollars.

Communications Equipment and Services Corporations

COMSHARE
Supplies computer, data and voice services through existing telecommunications networks. 1980 turnover: 71 million dollars.

CONTINENTAL TELEPHONE
Operates independent telephone systems in United States and Canada. Uses satellite of part-owned American Satellite. 1980 turnover: 1.3 billion dollars.

GRAPHIC SCANNING
Operates data communications network through rented telecommunications facilities; also telex and radio paging services. 1980 turnover: 43 million dollars.

ITT COMMUNICATIONS
Part of ITT. Largest international telex network in the United States. Operates a long distance telephone network, Cititel, in the United States. Sells communications equipment. 1980 turnover: 7.2 billion dollars.

MCI COMMUNICATIONS
Operates independent long distance telephone service between 100 plus US cities. 1980 turnover: 234 million dollars.

TYMSHARE
Largest US computer time-sharing company operating national and international data network. 1980 turnover: 236 million dollars.

UNITED TELECOMMUNICATIONS
Second largest (after GTE) US independent telephone company. Sells telephone equipment and data services. 1980 turnover: 1.9 billion dollars.

Background note 2
Value of Computer 'Fleets' Installed in Various Countries (1975)

Country/ Region	Value in Billions of Dollars	Per cent of machines of US Origin
United States	38.6	100
Canada	1.9	95
W. Europe	19	84
Socialist Countries	2.5	5
Japan	6.1	47
Others	1.9	84

Source: A. D. Little (*Le Sicob*, Le Monde, Sept. 18, 1975).

Background note 3
How AT & T and IBM lead the field

October 1981:
IBM launches, for the first time, a line of micro-computers (personal computers) in the new and highly competitive '16 bit' range. Also announces it will sell 'direct to the retail public' through Chase Manhattan bank branches, its own shops, agents and department stores.

December 1981:
AT & T announces a new two-way video service called Picturephone Meeting Service available in 16 cities in 1982 and 42 cities by the end of 1983. The service will compete with the Satellite Business System (IBM) service of teleconferencing.

February 1982:
AT & T announces it will begin sales of data- and word-processing systems under its own or another subsidiary name, foreshadowing the sale of small office computers for connection to AT & T PABX units in 1983.

February 1982:
IBM announces initiation of IBM Information Network. This will allow customers in seven major US cities to rent time on IBM computers in its Tampa, Florida computer centre. First it will offer computing time and 100 general financial programmes; later it plans to add data communications and electronic mail.

March 1982:
AT & T sets up two data-processing centres in Florida and New Jersey. The facilities are to be part of a proposed computer time-sharing, data/information network called Advanced Communications Service (ACS). Set to go into operation by the end of 1982.

April 1982:
AT & T completes acquisition of 45 per cent of Irish telecommunications manufacturer Telectron. Aims to sell equipment in Europe starting with digital radio systems – said to carry digital transmissions more efficiently than glass fibre cables.

April 1982:
AT & T opens London-based subsidiary AT & T International, a public company quoted on the London stock exchange. Announces it will seek finance for European projects on Euro-money markets.

April 1982:
AT & T's Western Electric begins marketing UNIX operating system for micro-computers – particularly '16 bit' units. The operating system allows exchange of software between a wide range of machines, including larger, faster '32 bit' machines. This is already accepted as the standard operating system for Japanese machines and is expected to become standard for most kinds of computers.

44

Background note 4
The big Ten Cable Companies

Merger and acquisition fever, coupled with bitter competition to gain local franchises in major American cities, took off around 1979. The trick is to get 'density': most 'Multi-System' operators feel they will begin to turn a profit when they are selling three or more 'subscription' channels to an average of 80,000 subscribers.

In 1982 there were an estimated 20 million cabled televisions in the United States. The ten companies listed here hold between them half that total. But as the larger companies (Warner Amex, Teleprompter and ATC) expand, cabling more households, the concentration shown here should intensify.

1. Teleprompter *2 million + subscribers*

Teleprompter is the oldest of the very large cable systems, and most of its strength is in New York (Manhattan). The company's multinational interests include its ownership, with the Bank of Suez, of International Communications Systems, which runs the Multivision Company of France, its control of cable systems in Mexico and its world wide sales of cable installation services. It also owns 50% of the second largest Pay-TV network. Showtime.

In 1980, Teleprompter was purchased outright by the Westinghouse Corporation. Westinghouse owns five television stations in the United States (with a weekly 8.6 million viewers – 12 per cent of US households), nine radio stations – and through its subsidiary supplies and syndicates programmes to many of America's radio stations. Group W has now joined with the Walt Disney Corporation and the American Broadcasting Corporation to form three Pay-TV programme networks: the 'Disney Channel' will offer recycled Disney productions and new offerings for the youth market and Group W-ABC will provide two 24-hour all news channels.

Westinghouse itself is the fifth largest electronics manufacturer in the United

States and also owns Linguaphone, the world's largest audio-visual language teaching corporation. The majority of shares in Westinghouse are held by the Mellon-First National Bost group of banks.

2. American TV and Communications (ATC) *1.8 million + subscribers*

ATC was purchased in 1978 by Time Inc., which also owns two large Pay-TV companies – Home Box Office (60 per cent of the US market) and Telemation.

Time Inc. is best known as the largest magazine publisher in the United States. It owns Time magazine itself as well as Fortune, Life, Money, People Weekly and Sports Illustrated With its 1977 purchase of the Book-of-the-Month Club, it also became the largest US publisher. Up to 30 per cent of its income comes from forestry and papermaking subsidiaries, including the jointly owned Eastex newsprint company. Through a Telefilm production company, Time Inc. has first call on all BBC productions offered to the USA.

3. Tele-Communications Inc. (TCI) *1.6 million subscribers*

TCI is unique in the top ten in not having cross-connections to other media conglomerates. It has reached its position simply by acquiring many small local systems in the Western United States and rural regions – 850 in the last five years. Unwilling to re-wire or modernise its systems, the company is seen as a speculator in the value of the cable subscribers themselves, likely to become an increasingly saleable commodity as cable density increases.

Most of the systems TCI has purchased have older coaxial cables only made to deliver 12 to 24 channels. Municipal councils are now demanding 80 to 100 channel capacities, which TCI has been unwilling or unable to build, and at least one city council (Boulder, Colorado) has taken TCI to court over this issue.

Many of the licences to operate which

TCI inherited when it bought the old little systems also come up for renewal in the next three years. Franchise battles are likely as hungry cable conglomerates look for more subscribers, sparking a final round of bitter confrontation between media companies.

4. Cox Communications *1 million subscribers*

Cox Communications owns five television stations with a weekly viewing audience of 4.5 million – 6 per cent of US households. It also owns six radio stations and is the tenth largest daily newspaper publisher. The company was all but purchased in 1980 by General Electric. The FCC then blocked the move, but might yet approve.

5. Warner Amex Cable Communications *1 million subscribers*

Linking Warner Communications and American Express, this has been one of the most aggressive companies in the competition for new urban franchises. It also owns the third largest Pay-TV network, The Movie Channel, and is pioneering the Qube 'interactive' cable TV system.

Warner Communications is itself owned by one of the largest US conglomerates, the Kinney Corporation, whose interests include funeral parlours, car parks and supermarket chains. Under Kinney, Warner Communications is divided into five groups: Books (including comic books and paperbacks); Leisure (including Warner Brothers/Seven Arts, fourth largest film company in the world, and Warner Records); Educational (especially TV material); Jungle Habitat (rival to Disneyland); American Express (banking, insurance and travel).

6. Times-Mirror Cablevison *600,000 subscribers*

Times-Mirror is a major media conglomerate with interests in newspapers, magazines, books and television. It is the eighth largest newspaper publisher in the United States (Los Angeles Times, Newsday,

etc.), owns two television stations, a batch of consumer magazines with a combined annual circulation of 75 million and a number of paperback publishers, including New English Library. In 1981 the company launched a Pay-TV movie channel, Spotlight, jointly owned by a number of cable companies, including Cox and TCI.

7. Sammons Communications *500,000 subscribers*

Sammons is a thrusting media company from Dallas, Texas, which decided recently to expand into cable television. It has small holdings in broadcasting and publishing.

8. Storer Cable Communications *500,000 subscribers*

Storer interests are in broadcasting and airlines: it owns seven TV stations and seven radio stations as well as a major shareholding in the Atlanta-based Delta Airlines. Storer has been competing aggressively for new cable franchises and recently completed a bitter court battle over Minneapolis with US Cablesystems.

9. Viacom International Inc. *500,000 subscribers*

Viacom was created by the *Columbia Broadcasting System (CBS)* in the 1960s to handle its cable interests as well as worldwide distribution of CBS programmes, video-cassettes and research into optical fibre communications. CBS was forced to divest itself of Viacom when, in 1970, the FCC adopted rules barring television networks from owning cable systems. These were recently lifted, however, and CBS was granted leave to purchase cable systems of less than 90,000 subscribers. This is considered the thin edge of the wedge, and there is speculation that CBS will move to repurchase Viacom. Viacom also owns 50 per cent of the second largest Pay-TV service, Showtime.

10. UA Cablesystems Ltd. *500,000 subscribers*

UA Cablesystems was renamed in 1981 when it was purchased by the dominant Canadian cable company, Rogers Cablesystems (see Chapter 2).

Background note 5
Pay-TV in the United States

Pay-TV is essentially the delivery of a series of programmes to cable television operators. It was always possible. One company, Telemation (Time Inc.), has been doing it for decades. But satellites mean they can be delivered cost-effectively to thousands of cable systems at the same time.

There are an estimated 4,000 cable systems in the United States today, and a lot of 'networks' competing for those markets. Competition is so stiff that some companies are paying cable operators to take their services. This is because, although the number of cable-fed televisions is expected to rise to 40 million by 1985, many of these systems do not have large channel capacities. But the number of 'networks' distributing their programmes by satellite is expanding very fast indeed. Most of these networks need to have a guaranteed audience of 500,000 before they can attract advertising or make cost-effective deals with programme producers. Thus the need to pay cable operators to make sure their schedule of programmes is offered.

Time Inc. towers over the Pay-TV industry. It owns both the largest and fourth largest networks – Home Box Office and Cinemax.

The Contenders
Home Box Office (Time Inc.) Carries movies (many from Columbia Pictures, now in the making) and a selection of Broadway plays, variety specials and original programmes, including those under exclusive contact from the British Broadcasting Corporation.
Showtime (Owned jointly by Teleprompter/Westinghouse and Viacom International) Offers the same sort of fare as HBO.
The Movie Channel (Warner/Amex) Movies.
Cinemax (Time Inc.) Movies.
Nickelodeon (Warner/Amex) Children's programmes.
ESPN (Getty Oil) Twenty-four hour sports.
Cable News Network (Turner Broadcasting) Twenty-four hour news.
Public Affairs Network News.

Spotlight (Cox Broadcasting Storer Broadcasting TCI Times-Mirror Cable) Same fare as HBO.

The Disney Channel (Westinghouse Walt Disney Corporation) Children's programming.

Satellite News Channels I and II (ABO Video Enterprises and Westinghouse News.

ARTS (Hearst Newspapers/ABC Video Enterprises) 'up-market' variety performance.

Daytime (Hearst Newspapers/ABC Video Enterprises). 'Women's' programming.

There are also a number of minority and special interest programme networks. Religious organisations are deeply involved, everyone from the Catholic Church to individual fundamentalist Christian preachers, for example the National Black Network, Christian Brothers Network, Spanish International Network.

Chapter 2
Canada: the most 'wired' nation on earth

When President Reagan's Ambassador in Ottawa recently made a series of speeches in which he celebrated the close ties between the 'peoples' of the two adjacent nations, there was a sting in the tail. 'I've talked to people out West, and they're not happy about this government's nationalist policies,' he said. 'What's going on here is just not playing by the free trade rules we've shared for so many years. The sad thing is that it's hurting you more than us.' Such forthright opinions on the Canadian government's trade and investment restrictions raised immediate eyebrows in parliament. This was not what they expected to hear from a close and trusted neighbour. To the business community, however, the Ambassador was swiftly hailed as the most realistic envoy to be sent North of the border for decades.

Canada is to all intents and purposes completely integrated into the Greater North American economy. It bore the full brunt of turn-of-the-century corporate expansion and has been the main target for United States overseas investment ever since. More money is now pumped into Canada by American companies than into the whole of Europe.

A very large, very empty hunk of geography (rivalling the Soviet Union in size), its population is, by comparison, small, and strung out in a series of urban oases and hamlets nestled close to the United States border. The nation lives by the sale of its natural resources, and most of these are owned by foreign companies. It has tried to build up its own industries, to create a local economy capable of selling finished goods at home and abroad. But the need to maintain its natural resource income means policies which make it easy for foreign companies to move capital and infrastructure in and out of the country. On the other hand, the desire to have internally-generated economic growth means policies which restrict the operation of foreign companies.

The political history of Canada revolves around these contradictory positions. They have emerged as 'continentalism' and 'nationalism', and have been espoused variously by every political party at every level. They have also cast a shadow over any serious economic planning. As one government economist put it: 'We have libraries full of research showing us exactly what conditions affect every sector. Strident recommendations abound, but when it comes to action there is always compromise. The circle takes another turn. The simple fact is that when you're so integrated into someone else's economy it's going to hurt someone when you try to move away.'

Computer-communications is no different from any other sector in the way it has been treated by Canada. What makes it interesting is that the country's particular history and geography has made communications a national priority since the nation's first days of semi-independence in 1867.

At the end of the last century, parliament decided that a 'regulatory body' was the best way of ensuring everybody got a piece of the action. The idea was that the government would defend the 'national interest' by stipulating how communications would be developed. Private industry would take it from there. In 1968, a Broadcasting Act specifically stipulated that firstly, 'the Canadian broadcasting system should be effectively owned and controlled by Canadians'. And secondly, that 'the programming provided by each broadcaster should be of high standard, using predominantly Canadian creative and other resources'.

But the contradictions in this were well summed up by a speech made in November 1978 by John Roberts, Canada's Secretary of State, at the UNESCO General Assembly in Paris. It was a fiery oration. He said that the Canadian government was deeply disturbed by UNESCO's shift towards encouraging government control over communications development. 'Canadians do not believe that either politicians or public servants should have anything to say in the management, direction or correction of the media,' he said.

The international media, particularly from the United States, covered Roberts' speech with much enthusiasm. Here, at last, was a strong voice raised in support of the unhindered development of media systems amongst the angry babble of Third World voices calling for control. It sounded like an endorsement of the 'free flow of information' position taken by the United States in the UNESCO debate. But after his speech Roberts held a press conference. At this, he condemned the US tactic of 'dumping' film and television programmes over the border and said that Canada needed to protect its cultural interests when threatened by products from a stronger economy. Afterwards, one reporter observed that his response 'was identical to Tunisian Ambassador Masmoudi's stand – that is, government must control what is shown by the media in order to protect the domestic culture'. Roberts was caught in a trap. Canadian policy seemed to be moving in two different directions at once.

How the regulators (try) to regulate

John Meisel came to Canada with his family from Czechoslovakia in 1942. He went to Toronto University, took a degree in politics and became a university lecturer. He has written and broadcast extensively about the Canadian political system. He knows the contradiction. He is a nationalist.

At the beginning of 1980 Meisel was appointed head of the Canadian Radio Television and Telecommunications Commission (CRTC), the latest in a long line of regulating bodies. He took his job seriously. He wanted Canada's media – radio and TV especially – to live up to the notions of communications sovereignty enshrined in government policy, and to give those ideas regulatory force. 'The CRTC is not quite as much of a patsy as it seems,' he is quoted as saying, 'and we're going to toughen up even more.'

Some people think he's a fool. 'It's a beautiful, charming idea to turn Canadian eyes back on to ourselves,' commented one communications analyst. 'But it's out of touch with the audience. There is no border in broadcasting and Canadian audiences don't listen to the CRTC. Now is not the time for Canadian nationalism in broadcasting. We're into a new international age, and the CRTC can't be policeman anymore.'

Even those close to the CRTC believe that it never stood a chance. For whether or not the Commission regulates, the communications companies have always seemed to do pretty much what they liked. One CRTC consultant gloomily cited the example of the Canadian telephone system.

'At the turn of the century the government decided it needed a nation-wide telecommunications system,' he explained. 'Bell got the nod. But instead of taking on the whole cake it picked up the nice bits, the areas showing the most promise of being lucrative in the future. These were mainly in the East, between Montreal and Toronto. The rest of the country was left to fend for itself. What emerged was a phone network dominated by Bell telephone, with a gaggle of small systems ending out West in British Columbia where the network came to be controlled by the US firm General Telephone and Electric.

'The government said it wanted to build up a strong Canadian telecom-munications corporation when it allowed Bell its money-spinning monopoly. But the firm was all but wholly owned by the American corporation AT & T until the US Congress forced its sale in 1956. Even after that they were so intertwined through patents and management contracts things stayed much the same. Bell, GTE (posing as British Columbia Telephone) and the welter of smaller provincial companies eventually formed themselves into a network and association called Trans-Canada Telephone System (TCTS). The American Bell Corpora-tion controlled more than 60 per cent of the equity. And over the years Bell would go to the government for permission to raise rates or change the services offered by TCTS. After a bit of huffing and puffing they got what they asked for. Pretty soon they were acting like a law unto them-selves. I think it was about then that the regulatory bodies lost control of the Canadian communications system.'

This saga has also set the tone for the computer-communications which followed. Telesat, for example, the company responsible for Cana-dian communications satellites, was originally established as a public corporation in 1969 by an Act of Parliament. Twelve years later, how-ever, Telesat is part of TCTS, stripped of government control, and complaining about the mass of unnecessary regulations. (See background note 1.)

'Something like that can happen here because the Federal government makes laws to enforce the national interest, said the CRTC consultant, 'then changes them in practice to support local private monopolies or help Canadian companies produce for the US market place. In the midst of this double-think the hapless CRTC, and a clutch of regulatory agen-cies set up to make those nationalist laws work, are hopelessly compro-mised. Every time someone takes their regulating job seriously they get pilloried.

'Canada has scored all sorts of firsts. We've got some of the top experts in the world and we're one of the few nations with our own space industry. (See background note 2.) Yet now you go to com-puter-communications conferences and everyone's complaining that we've fallen behind the rest of the industrialised world. I suppose you have to ask what our national interest really is.'

The most 'wired' nation on earth

*Edward Rogers, chief executive of Rogers Cablesystems – the largest mul-
tiple systems operator in the world – seemed unworried as he announced
that his firm would take a loss during the year 1982. 'We've spent a lot of
money getting into the United States,' he said briskly. 'The 1982 budget for
franchise competitions alone is three million dollars. Once we've reached a
million subscribers it'll be time to ease off. Earnings will take off around
1985. That will be the harvest year.'*

Canadians have been hooking their televisions up to cables since 1953,
and Rogers Cablesystems has grown by buying the systems as they
spread. Television owners were willing to pay an average of six dollars a
month to watch US commercial programmes captured on aerials nudging
the border, in the process making government rules for Canadian content
in television programmes redundant.

From the early 1950s, when cable television first got underway, until
1968, when the CRTC finally got its hands on the medium, there was no
regulation beyond the requirement to obtain a receiver licence from the
Department of Transport. And by the time CRTC started investigating
cable, in the late 1960s, the industry was already the fastest growth area
of communications in Canada. It had upwards of two million customers,
it was doubling its audience potential every four years and it had made
Canada the most 'wired' nation on earth. The limits of subscriber density
were fast approaching, and cable was competing for revenues against
broadcast television in most major markets.

For a little over 15 years cable was in fact the only area of Canadian
broadcasting unfettered by any public scrutiny of its activities. And the
profits could be massive: a 40 per cent rate of return was not unheard of.
In most cases the average return rate was 24 per cent – compared to an
average for television broadcasting of 13 per cent.

The wildcat nature of the industry attracted large private media
capital, and from its inception the trend was towards concentration.

One example of concentration is the Premier company, which in 1976
controlled 13 per cent of all cable systems. By 1980 that company had
been amalgamated with the second largest, Canadian Cablesystems, and
under the ownership of a third, Rogers Cablesystems, to control 1.3
million subscribers. In addition, Rogers moved aggressively into the
United States, buying cable systems in the mid-West as well as a controlling interest in UA Columbia cable systems (the tenth largest cable sup-
plier in America). By 1980, 75 per cent of all Canadian household had
access to cable services. And throughout this period of phenomenal
growth one assumption underwrote every cable industry justification:
Canadian people want uncensored United States programming.

The economic argument behind this is simple. Because its market is
larger than Canada's, United States television has has been able to spend
more on production. Volume production and volume sales make for
cheap prices, whilst producers in Canada have less to spend because their
market and income are both smaller. So Canadian TV programmers find
it more profitable to buy programmes (in the case of cable they are free
for the pulling from over the border) cheap from the United States than
put up money for distinctive local productions of good technical quality.

United States programming isn't just cheap, it also 'looks more professional'. Once the consumer believes that the professionality alone of the foreign product is the measure for national programming, it doesn't take much to believe that US programmes are somehow better, more what TV should really be like. When these popularly-held ideas are further challenged by a government agency whose sole mechanism for encouraging national programming is to stop people seeing 'Dallas' and 'Kojak', access to that foreign programming become an issue of freedom of choice, a matter of conscience.

The cable companies successfully used this argument to keep the CRTC out of any discussion of cable throughout the 1960s, particularly in the Canadian parliament. It was a neat combination of the 'national' theme and the 'free-flow' theme. In the end, the CRTC left programming alone and went for protection of local Canadian broadcasters. The cable companies were told to substitute local commercials in programmes beamed in from the South and to make 'levelling-off' payments to Canadian television broadcast companies.

The CRTC also 'encouraged' cable operators to offer channels for local community broadcasting, on the condition that this was asked for by local communities. The companies in turn said they couldn't afford to do this until they had achieved economies of scale. But even after concentration had reached unprecedented proportions in the 1970s one CRTC investigator found that the amount of money spent on local programming was unaffected. Cable companies were just skimming the cream.

One sign of the ruthless nature of the cable business, and the determination of the major companies to ensure total control, is the practice of 'trafficking' in franchise licences. This means that when one company sells out to another they exploit the loopholes in current legislation so they can designate who is to receive the franchise licence. There is then no new competition when that licensee is bought out. The result has been that very few community-access cable TV systems have got underway in Canada. At the last count there were barely three or four, mostly in rural Western regions where the cost of cabling-up is high.

The CRTC did in fact investigate a mass of complaints that a community-cable group hadn't had a look-in during one of Rogers Cablesystems' take-over operations. But although the complaints went to the Department of Communications, back to the CRTC, even to the Canadian cabinet, the government eventually said it could do nothing. No change was made in the licence application procedure.

At the same time as the licensing scandal, however, the Canadian cable system started to reach densities which made it useless for a growing company to bother selling new systems. So where would they go from there? 'The information revolution came along just in time,' said one industry analyst. 'It was pretty clear what the strategy would be. When you're looking at a subscriber base here yielding six dollars a month per unit, and South of the border the largest television market in the world is going bananas for cable at an average rate of 30 dollars a month, you take your bread and head South. But those Canadian systems are not going to be money spinners forever. That's the beauty of interactive and pay cable TV. You can sell them as a tiered service. If you're lucky you've got a coaxial that carries at least 24 channels. Bingo, you can start selling add-ons and maybe quadruple that six bucks a month.'

Pay-TV: more of the same

Zena Cherry is a society and gossip columnist for the Toronto Globe and
Mail. *She moves in high circles – lunching with concert pianists, hobnob-
bing with diplomats, luxuriating on Caribbean beaches with millionaires.
On the morning of March 22, 1982 she had to report on a different sort of
event.*

'*It was an evening of excitement as Canadian television history was
being made,' she wrote. 'It was a nine o'clock party, and for the first part
of the evening there was a buffet of smoked salmon, paté, Parma ham,
veal meatballs and spinach quiche, all catered in a flash by Phillipe Joyet,
formerly of Sutton Place. The host's parents were there and his father,
G. Cyril (Gus) Harris, supervisor of estimating services for Toronto Hydro,
gave a charming upbeat toast to Steven, Judith and Superchannel.*'

The event which warranted such culinary detail in the Toronto society
columns was the arrival of Pay Cable television, and Gus Harris' son
Steven was the head of Ontario Independent Pay Television – one of six
companies licensed to sell programmes to subscribers. (See background
note 3.) But not everyone was as sycophantic as Zena Cherry about the
prospect. 'For all these companies to break even selling Canadian-made
programmes, subscribers will have to take at least two services,' wrote
one disgruntled commentator. 'Only in Toronto, Calgary and Vancouver
is there a snowball's chance in hell that more than a handful of subscribers will do that. With decoding hardware to link in your TV costing 18
to 20 dollars to rent on top of ten to 20 a month for each service it's a
non-starter. Who'll pay that? All those unemployed Canadians in the
Atlantic provinces? Canadians in Quebec? For a service that originates
outside Quebec from a company neither of whose principals is a
Quebecker or speaks French?' There's a simple answer. The services will
sell programmes made in the United States, particularly Hollywood
telefilms. It will be more of the same.

When the CRTC first called for applications for pay-TV, it laid special
emphasis on licensing companies ready to provide distinctive Canadian
programming. Predictably, the cable companies had a different view.
They said that the only reason for pay-TV was so that Canadians could
gain access to the services developing in the United States. They wanted
each operator to have complete freedom to offer whichever programmes
they cared to select from the Canadian subscription services. They got
that. The ones providing US programmes will also be the cheapest.

As one observer at the CRTC hearings pointed out: 'The cable people
see the US movie channels as the pump-primers which will bring in the
cash that might later provide for Canadian productions. It's an argument
we've seen before when the CRTC was trying to make them set aside
money for local access channels. It just didn't happen. There is no reason
to believe it would happen now. That's why a bunch of film-makers'
associations appealed to the cabinet to overturn the CRTC decisions.'

The film-makers argued that Canadian producers will be squeezed
between foreign film suppliers, on whom the licensees will depend for
product and the cable companies, on whom they will depend for access to
the audience. The result would be a drop in money available for Canadian productions, with Pay Cable simply adding to the marginalisation of
local programming.

54

One lawyer working for the cable television companies brought the argument full circle and re-affirmed that the CRTC's notions of national cultural policies in a corporate age were irrelevant. 'We must give up this cultural sovereignty nonsense,' he said, 'and recognize that Canada and the US are one single entertainment market just as they are one single automobile market. As long as we maintain a satisfactory level of employment in the television industry what does it matter whether we make 'American' shows or 'Canadian' ones? There is really so little difference as to be immaterial.' The cabinet itself was caught between the age-old desire for independence and the impossibility of breaking its economic ties with America. So it ruled accordingly. There would be no change to the CRTC decision.

A flea on the American dog

'When a company like IBM makes a move you've got to get worried,' said the Toronto computer time-sharing salesman. 'The time-sharing and data network services here are like a flea on the American dog. The dog is IBM. When they announced they were going to begin selling computer services again we all went stiff with terror. For years we've been nestling in at the margins of the computer-communications industry. Wherever the big people are not interested, Canadian companies have sprung up to take a profit. It means we're big on PABX systems, software, computer time-sharing services, a few end-bits for micros – and little else. This deregulation thing in the US is going to change all that.' (See background note 4.)

It will change because Canada has an open data and computer technologies border with the United States. No one has cared or had the political will to change that. In practice, this means that it's cheaper to attach your phone to a US network for voice/data services than look around for a (more expensive) Canadian service. And although Canada has developed some of its own on-line information services, such as Statistics Canada's CANSIM data base and the National Research Council's automated bibliographic service CISTI, the fact remains that data services from the United States are swamping any notion of independent development. Most Canadian business, banking and even some government files are now on US data bases.

'We've had Royal Commissions on the problem,' said a CRTC insider. 'They've called for a rounded approach, limiting the extent to which we're locked into the US information system, but, you know, these computer-communications corporations are nearly all American, they're serving a corporate structure that's almost all American, and together they provide a ministry by ministry lobby that's pretty hard to ignore. (See box: Transborder Flow.)

Transborder Flow into Canada

In 1977 a government study was made of 400 US-based companies operating in Canada to establish the level of cross-border data flow. The information gathered indicated that the value of computing services imported into Canada would amount to some 300-350 million dollars in 1978 . . . it was estimated that by 1985 the value of imported computer services will have increased to about 1.5 billion dollars. It was further estimated that, as a result, some

23,000 directly related jobs will have been lost to the Canadian economy by that time.' (Report of the Consultative Committee on the Implication of Telecommunications and Canadian Sovereignty, 1979.)

The Committee recommended 1. That government require data processing related to Canadian business operations be performed in Canada; 2. That the Bank Act be revised to prohibit the export of client data; 3. That finance structures be treated in such a way as to give greater access to risk capital for Canadian corporations in data processing; 4. That the government promote training schemes for programmers, systems analysts and others required for developing Canadian systems.

A Department of Communications 'Interdepartmental Task Force' is now taking evidence from various interested parties on the problem of transborder data flows. Examples of the reaction so far range from the Canadian Business Equipment Manufacturers Association (includes the Canadian subsidiaries of most large US-based computer multinationals) – which argues that 'The continued free flow of information across national boundaries is essential to the health and growth of the Canadian economy' – to the Canadian Independent Computer Services Association (represents Canadian-owned computer/data information service companies) – which argues that because computers and telecommunications costs are considerably lower in the United States, a decision not to restrict data flow would lead to US domination of Canada's information processing industry. The Canadian Association of Data Processing Services Organisations represents private and public agencies and a cross-section of Canadian professionals in the area has called for legislation to ensure data relating to Canadian citizens be kept in Canada and that Canada's Foreign Investment Review Agency monitor the activities of foreign data/information services.

'What we say we *want* to do, particularly at international meetings like the OECD Cross-Border Data Flow get-togethers, is very different from what's actually happening. In the end the government seems to be picking a few areas where there is a bit of native expertise and a chance to compete on a world market. Once they've got that they just start throwing money around. It's happened with PABX systems, it's happened with micro-computers, and it's happening with Telidon. I suppose the logic is that if you're so far gone that computer-communications is going to take you the last step into someone else's economy you may as well go for the main chance inside that arena.'

Telidon is an interesting example. 'In one sense you could say it all comes down to electronic publishing,' said the information salesman sitting in an Ottawa bar. 'The government has come up with a winner in Telidon. They've got a technology second to none. But they can't find a market for it, and it's running foul of the competition between the phone system and the cable television companies. It's expensive for all but the business community, and those people are going in droves for micro-computers they can hook up to US data/information networks. I suppose it's the same old story: we pour millions into a national product and then hold our breath to see if it will fit into the North American market place. If it does it gets sold back to us from the United States.' (See box: Why Telidon is better.)

Why Telidon is better

Canada's 'second generation' videotext technology arrived on the scene seven years after the original, Britain's Prestel. The Canadian system is 'alphageometric': this means it can 'plot' a line mathematically, by geometric co-ordinants, and then 'draw it out' on the screen. The result is 'high resolution' or 'smooth' graphics. Prestel, by contrast, is 'alphamosaic': this means that the chip masterminding graphics can only construct images through a series of single linear computations. The result appears on the screen like building blocks or a mosaic.

In addition, Telidon uses coding systems which, unlike Prestel, make it independent of the display system used (the TV set) and the method of transmission (phone line, cable, optical fibre). This gives both consumers and information providers great flexibility in choosing equipment and creating data bases. It is also a means of keeping pace with technical innovation, allowing for both 'backward' and 'forward' capability. Forward capability means the system has been designed so that future terminals can access old data; backward capability means that existing terminals will be able to receive information from data bases established in the future.

The Canadian approach to stimulating videotext also differs from the British and French. For whilst the latter schemes, like Prestel, have been implemented through the countries' national phone systems, Canada has approved a number of provincial projects, with the private sector determining the ultimate success of each one. By Spring 1982 there were 52 Telidon experiments in action, ranging from one service in Manitoba – offering interactive information on weather patterns and the price of corn to farmers – to single units in shopping precincts.

'The problem,' said one computer magazine editor, 'is the information. There just isn't enough of it floating around to make Telidon interesting. One system in Ottawa is offering suburban shoppers 33,000 'pages' of information on government programmes. That's because they've sought the advice of various cliques of academics, educators and librarians. They couldn't have picked a population less knowledgeable about the tastes of the average Canadian unless they'd appointed a panel of Federal bureaucrats. What that bunch has been serving up as broccoli has long since been recognized as spinach – and the public says to hell with it.'

The business community is an equally hard sell, so much so that the largest experiment, operated in the Toronto area, has been handed over by the original agency, Bell Canada, to a private company, Infomart, owned by a group of Canadian newspapers. But even Infomart is finding it difficult to get advertising sponsors for what is essentially a public information system.

Cost is another problem. In 1982 a Telidon unit cost 2,000 dollars. It could drop as low as 800 dollars by the end of 1983, with a convertor for a normal television an extra 300 dollars. But a 1980 study by the Department of Communications found a household would need an income of 37,000 dollars a year in 1985 to afford a 25 dollar a month Telidon service. The average Canadian income peaks somewhere around 12–15,000 dollars a year. Not surprisingly, the DoC report estimated that the Canadian home audience in 1985 would probably be about 13,000.

Infomart sees it as a 'chicken and egg' problem. Potential providers of information and services are waiting for a large audience before committing themselves, while Telidon manufacturers cannot come up with the huge investment required to develop a custom-made silicon chip – crucial to mass production – until more services are available.

Bell Canada, meanwhile, has moved on to what it sees as more profitable territory. Instead of experimenting with Telidon technologies it has concentrated on providing an information network 'that you can hook up anything to.' So in July 1982, the company launched a new data/information network through the Bell-controlled Trans-Canada Telephone System. Called Inet, it's being sold as the 'gateway' for either Telidon terminals or micro-computers to receive already existing services on both sides of the border. So far, the user can access six data services as well as the computerised files of the *Toronto Globe and Mail*, the Canadian Press Wires service, the *Financial Post of Canada* and the *New York Times*.

'Let's face it,' said the Infomart salesman, 'the micro-computer is cheaper and more flexible, a proven tool. They cost as little as 300 dollars. The market for them doubled between 1981 and 1982. Computer companies expect to sell a million by 1985. You can get it tailored to your own needs. Anyone trying to sell Telidon terminals has got to take this into consideration.'

One group with this in mind are the cable TV operators, with Rogers Cablesystems leading the way. In 1981 the company announced it was purchasing Telidon display and image creating terminals to enhance programming in the Toronto area. This means that although Telidon still doesn't reach its hoped-for mass audience, the system's graphics will be used by Rogers to enhance the company's teletext service. But before Rogers can go one step further – and start selling keyboards to make a one-way teletext service into a two-way viewdata service – they have another problem: Bell's monopoly of the telephone cables.

In Canada, the telephone companies own the poles on which the co-axial cables are strung. These companies, led by Bell, have made the cable firms sign contracts which stipulate that they can't be used to run interactive information services of any kind. To date, not even the CRTC has seemed ready to confront Bell.

The Commission *has* made two suggestions. One would follow the lead of the Federal Communications Commission in the United States, removing the telephone companies completely from cable TV by requiring them to provide reasonable pole attachment rights and forbidding them to own coaxial cable for cable TV purposes. Another would confirm sole ownership of all cables to the telephone companies but forbid them from offering any possible cable TV service. Neither option has so far been accepted by either side.

At least the salesman from Infomart will be happy. His Telidon-based information system might be easier to sell now, especially since AT & T has established it as the standard for its proposed mass viewdata system. This happened in July 1982. It just might save Telidon; it certainly saved

58

the Canadian companies licensed to produce Telidon technology. But there is a catch. AT & T has just accepted the design, not the hardware. As an AT & T spokesman admitted: Deregulation will allow consumers to connect their telephone lines to any compatible computer-communications devices they wish. And there's no guarantee AT & T will buy from Canadian companies. Canadians have no patent on the technolgy.'

Bucking a trend

CRTC boss, John Meisel, still feels the Canadian interest should be uppermost in communications regulation: 'One of the disasters of this country is that we've spent too much time copying American forms. We should be able to show what differences there are in being Canadian.'

He's a man bucking a trend. In every area of computer-communications the private sector believes the best way to make the information revolution Canadian is to become as American as possible – and they've got half the government playing their tune. The president of the government-sponsored Communications Satellite corporation says the only way to make satellites work for Canada is to do it the American way. The cable TV industry, with its new side-kicks from Pay-TV, are ready to live or die by selling American programmes, preferably in the US market. Other government departments have already accepted a future for computer hardware and software systems integrated totally into the US corporate market. Even the videotext people, pushing a world-beating technology, are loathe to have a state-sponsored information system built around it for Canadians, and are prepared to let AT & T set the pace of development.

One of Meisel's latest headaches is 2,000 illegal satellite dishes dotted around Canada, all pulling down television signals from US communications satellites. (See box: Satellite Crazy.) And he's also got Bell virtually deregulating itself so that it can move full tilt into the computer hardware and services market. This has been done by clever manipulation of its corporate structure.

Where does all this leave the effectiveness of Canadian government control of the new communications? In 1980, Robert Bebe, a communications consultant specialising in cable TV, delivered a report on CRTC rules for cable under contract from the Department of Communications. 'The licensing and regulatory authority, the CRTC,' he reported, 'has been given the mandate and authority to supervise the Canadian broadcasting system in such a way as to achieve the goals set for broadcasting. The CRTC itself believes it has failed in this task.'

Satellite Crazy

As soon as television could be received from satellities, Canadians started putting up receiving dishes to capture the US commercial channels. Today, there are as many as 2,000 dishes operating throughout the country, particularly in Northern areas and the more remote settlements. They are all illegal. Canadian law does not permit the private operation of a satellite dish aerial.

Many satellite receivers are simply for private use, but others are used by companies to sell programmes to people through cables. Some cable companies operate them right under the nose of the CRTC in Ontario.

'Ron Bothwekl, owner of the Satellite Connection in Mount Brydges near London, Ontario, said he is doing a landslide business in earth station hardware. He said a 12-foot dish and the necessary receiving equipment costs 6,200 dollars. "People don't care anymore whether it's illegal to operate a dish", he stated. "They want television entertainment, and they're willing to pay for it." ' (Toronto Globe and Mail, *Nov. 17, 1981.)*

The CRTC has tried in vain to put a stop to the proliferation of earth stations, and the issue has become, like cable television, a matter of 'free choice'. Its position has not been helped by the fact that, in many cases, municipal and provincial governments and the courts are working actively in support of the satellite stations. In a notable decision, a Newfoundland provincial judge ruled in 1981 that satellite reception and redistribution through cables did *not* constitute broadcasting in the sense that the Federal Broadcasting Act defines. As a result, a local cable operator was allowed to continue offering a US channel to his customers.

Almost every week the newspapers carry tongue-in-cheek stories of the crafty backwoods cable operator who has eluded the Federal 'satellite police' (as hapless Department of Transport inspectors are often called). In one area of Quebec the municipal council has an elaborate underground alert system to tell the cable operator when the forces of law are about to raid.

The CRTC is in a difficult position. It is handing out licenses to Canadian companies to provide Pay-TV via satellite at a price which will inevitably be higher because of the stipulations for the provision of Canadian content. At the same time, satellite operators are springing up around the country picking off US Pay Cable network programming *for nothing but the cost of their satellite.* Pirated US programming is certain to be cheaper than the product of the licensed Canadian companies.

Background notes

Background note 1
Telesat: A Chronology

1969:
Telesat Canada Act creates a public corporation to launch and operate satellites for Canada. Ownership to be apportioned between federal government, telecommunications carriers and general public. Act prohibits Telesat from entering into associations or partnerships which might compromise internal management control of all aspects of satellite development. Nearly half of the corporation's shares are taken up by telecommunications carriers; 50 per cent remains in government hands.

1972:
Telesat signs five-year service contracts with Trans Canada Telephone System (TCTS), Canadian National Canadian Pacific Telecommunications (CNCP) (the telex facilities of the two national railway systems), the Canadian Broadcasting Corporation (CBC) and Bell Canada.

Canada/US inter-governmental exchange of letters establishes principles and conditions for the use of each other's domestic satellite communications services.

1973:
Telesat provides satellite channel services to RCA Global Communications and RCA Alaska Communications – according to 1972 agreement with USA.

1974:
Telesat profits reach 3.6 million dollars, up from 1.6 million in 1973. The reasons are the RCA deal and CBC's 'accelerated coverage plan' to reach Northern and remote areas with television service.

1975:
RCA gets domestic communications satellite facility, closes Telesat arrangement. Telesat profits dip for the first time.

1976:
Telesat announces merger with Trans Canada Telephone System, becoming tenth member of the consortium. Reason given: need for financial security. A TCTS feasibility study has reported that a satellite system inaugurated by the consortium to run parallel to Telesat would be too costly. TCTS reason for merger: to acquire a satellite system. The letter of agreement includes these provisions: 'Designs shall be compatible with economic and performance requirements and with service plans as established by TCTS,' and that 'satellite system design concepts and other information (should) fully support TCTS planning activities and ensure optimum use of satellite facilities in the TCTS networks'.

Government Department of Communications makes these stipulations for the merger: 1. Telesat must continue in economic viability without public funds, although it would be accepted that Canadian citizens would subsidise Telesat R&D via high telephone rates. 2. Telesat must have equal standing to other members of TCTS. 3. Customers, particularly government departments, should be offered direct access to Telesat without going through TCTS. 4. Non-TCTS users may not be discouraged from using Telesat either by rate structures or administrative measures. 5. Agreement should not, in practise, jeopardise federal legislative or regulatory jurisdiction in the field of satellite communications.
CRTC objects to merger because it would undermine autonomy of decision-making within Telesat, in contravention of 1969 Telesat Canada Act. Also worried that government representation within Telesat (50 per cent) has been reduced to 0.5 of one vote out of ten on satellite systems development in TCTS. Merger might also create a private monopoly over satellite communications. Merger would seem to contravene Railway Act (under which CRTC must regulate

rates for communications services) by putting a national service inside the prerogative of a private operator whose rates may not be wholly regulated by CRTC.

1977:
Federal Cabinet upholds merger and rules in favour of Department of Communications guarantees. CRTC issues statement to the effect that it will have difficulty guarding against discrimination and adjudicating complaints. Private communications companies launch complaints: these include Canadian Press Wire Service, Broadcast News Service and Canadian Cable Television Association. They feel the merger will encourage discriminatory rates for services offered to non-TCTS users.

1977-80:
Telesat operates satellites with very little non-TCTS use. Only CBC and CNCP use whole channel facilities outside those allotted to TCTS users and federal government. Satellites orbit with spare capacity. Telesat begins to receive guaranteed income, according to agreement with TCTS, rising by one per cent a year.

1978:
Telesat awards contracts for the construction of three communications satellites. Anik B, world's first commercial dual band (6/4 GHz and 14/12 GHz) satellite successfully launched.

1980:
Telesat provides world's first commercial broadcast services in the 14/12 GHz frequency band (French language video programming for a consortium of Quebec cable television operators). CRTC committee on extension of services to remote and Northern communities recommends introduction of 'Pay-TV' and other services, to be carried on Telesat satellites. The same committee comments: 'Whether or not present and proposed rates for the use of satellite capacity can be justified, they are so high as to be an impediment to plans for the extension of broadcasting services.'

July 1981:
CRTC ends hearings on the relationship between Telesat and TCTS. Originally designed to rule on rate structures, these are quickly broadened into a wholesale attack on the Telesat-TCTS link by non-TCTS users.
The Complaints:
Non-TCTS members wanting to lease part of a channel were forced to deal through TCTS. The administrative structure of the association did not allow them to deal directly with Telesat, even when prepared to pay retail rates (as opposed to the 'wholesale' rates available to TCTS members). TCTS members were also at an 'unfair trading advantage' because they received half the income from Telesat over its guaranteed annual rate. CRTC investigators also report that Telesat executives consider TCTS to be the satellite facility's 'marketing and planning arm', in violation of the Telesat Canada Act. Business communications organisations complain that the Telesat price structure has forced them to use land-based transmission systems, even though satellite communications are cheaper. Representatives from Northern and remote communities say the rate structure of TCTS for satellite services is also restricting delivery of television and radio services: this has left many parts of the country without improved communications, even though this was the specific intention of the Telesat Canada Act.
The CRTC accepts many of these complaints, and stipulates a return to the situation before the merger of Telesat Canada and Trans Canada Telephone System, particularly that non-TCTS organisations can deal directly with Telesat for channel space.

December 1981:
Department of Communications 'varies' the CRTC decision to bar all but broadcasting organisations from dealing direct with Telesat. In all other matters it allows Telesat-TCTS arrangement to stand. In the same month, Telesat signs US to US service contract with Argo Communications Corporation (six channels to be rented).

February 1982:
Telesat Canada signs service agreement with General Telephone

and Electronics of the United States independent company.' – *Toronto Globe* and *Mail*, March 29, 1982. Eldon D. Thomson, President, Telesat Canada: 'Canada has lagged behind the United States and other countries not because of any market restrictions but because of regulatory constraints . . . the regulatory bodies have got to stop procrastinating and allow Canada to get on with what is now allowed in the United States.' *Toronto Globe* and *Mail*, March 29 1982.

(GTE Satellite Corporation) for rental of ten channels. The company will also carry signals for company rebroadcasting United States television to the Canadian arctic and North-West.

March 1982:
CRTC licenses two national and three regional Pay-TV networks. At least half these companies propose to rebroadcast US Pay-TV programming using the facilities of Telesat Canada (e.g. providing movies shown on Home Box Office – see Pay-TV section of chapter). But Telesat Canada has rented so much channel space to United States companies already, that special talks have to start on whether the space is available.

April 1982:
Telesat Canada signs interim service contract with Oak Satellites Corporation of California for use of four channels from June 1983. Telesat Canada and representatives of Pay-TV companies meet. 'Telesat offers to attempt to explore the possibility of arranging a six-month deferral of the start of the contracted US services on receipt of firm, written commitments by the potential Canadian customers of the Anik-C communications satellite to a service start-up date of not later than February 1, 1983.' (From Telesat press release, May 1982)

A Toronto media lawyer: 'The most cynical and appalling thing about the sales (of broadcasting channels to US companies) is that just before the July 1981 decision Telesat along with all the other TCTS cronies, filed a petition to cabinet, saying Telesat couldn't possibly survive as an independent company." *Toronto Globe and Mail*, March 29, 1982. Eldon D.

Thomson, President, Telesat Canada: "Canada has lagged behind the United States and other countries not because of any market restrictions but because of regulatory constraints . . . the regulatory bodies have got to stop procrastinating and allow Canada to get on with what is now allowed in the United States." – *Toronto Globe and Mail*, March 29, 1982.

Background note 2

Canada in Space

The Canadian government made an early commitment to satellite technology. In the 1960s it had notable successes with two series of atmospheric analysis units (Alouette and Isis), and has latterly sunk millions into the design and development of speciality communications satellites. In 1980/81 the Department of Communications spent the largest portion of its budget (27 per cent) on satellite communications, feeding in nearly 50 million dollars of direct and indirect investment. A further 476 million is earmarked up to 1985.

Canada's early investment in communications satellites also resulted in a number of technological 'firsts', including the first national geostationary communications satellite system and the first commercial direct broadcast service using the 14/12 GHz band. Experimentation is equally advanced in the use of direct broadcast satellites for social and medical services to remote communities, for delivery of educational television to remote areas and for special radio services, including maritime search and rescue. For some years, selected areas of Northern Canada have also been able to receive the two national television networks, and a good deal of telecommunications traffic has been travelling via satellites for more than a decade.

By 1985 Canada should have as many as eight communications satellites in orbit, capable of offering 100 channels (transponders). This compares to only 19 in early 1982.

Background note 3

Pay-TV Comes to Canada

In 1981 the CRTC invited applications to provide 'subscription television programming', better known as Pay-TV. Licences would be awarded in three categories: General Interest, Specialty and Multilingual programming.

A major stipulation for applicants was that they should provide a percentage of 'Canadian content' – both as a proportion of exhibition time and of expenditures. The 'General Interest' licencee, for example, would be expected to exhibit Canadian content programming for 30 per cent of its schedule, rising to 50 per cent after one year. It would also be expected to spend 60 per cent of its budget on Canadian programmes.

The applicants can be divided into two groups. The larger of these offered services to be purchased by the cable operator on a programme by programme basis. The subscriber would then choose to buy the channels on which the operator placed a selection of programmes for a fee in addition to the basic rental. The other group (only two of the applicants) proposed a 'universal channel'. This would be a part of the basic cable service, paid for by the operator. This both inferred a higher rental fee and would depend on making carriage of the whole channel mandatory for the operator.

The first group laid heavy emphasis on presentation of telefilms. They said Canadian content would average anywhere from 14 to 50 per cent. The second group emphasised original productions, predicting Canadian content well above 50 per cent of programming. Both companies in this group were non-profit, one with a co-operative structure. Neither received a licence.

Background note 4

United States Domination of Canadian Computer Industry

Top Computer Companies Operating in Canada

Company name	Ownership	Total revenues 1980 ($ million)
1. IBM Canada	US	1,506.3
2. Digital Equipment of Canada	US	163.7
3. Control Data Canada	US	162.6
4. NCR Canada	US	176.6
5. AES Data	Can.	155.0
6. Sperry	US	279.6
7. Philips Data Systems	Netherlands	100.3
8. Honeywell	US	262.5
9. Burroughs Business Machines	US	105.0
10. Canada Systems Group (EST)	Can.	77.9

After 1981 the Canadian government took steps to force foreign computer companies to direct more of their production into Canada. In a landmark case, the government's Foreign Investment Review Agency made Apple Computer Corporation agree to the construction of an assembly plant and to contribute some of its profits to the development of an institute for research and training of Canadian computer personnel.

Chapter 3
Europe: swimming against the US tidal wave?

In 1967 Jean-Jacques Servan Schreiber, the French politician and writer, shared a blinding insight with a receptive European public. Others were saying similar things, but none were as influential. American corporations were dominating the European economy, he said, and if this situation was allowed to continue Europe would fall permanently behind in the 'race for progress'.

In his book, 'The American Challenge' (1968), Servan Schreiber explained that the Americans had achieved their unassailable lead because they were able to initiate scientific and technological innovations and bring them to the market place through corporate economies of scale achieved by multinational mergers and diversification. He felt Europe could only hope to compete if it also laid heavy emphasis on science and technology research and development. He wanted national policies to encourage companies to become big enough to compete with the Americans. He said organisation on a European-wide scale would make this possible. Most importantly, Schreiber told Europeans they were losing out on the development and control of computer-communications, which he believed would be the engine of history after the year 2000.

It is difficult to convey the effect that this book had on the business intelligentsia of the period, especially in France. Schreiber was the man responsible for the success of L'Express magazine. As editor he had outraged the French army by calling for peace and independence in Algeria. What he was saying reshaped the patriotic notion of the French destiny. He was a man to listen to, and what he said was heard at the very top.

There were other people saying these things: in universities, research centres, and some parts of government. But here was an easy street level explanation for French and European technological backwardness: the Americans were to blame. And Schrieber was also suggesting frameworks which Europeans might use when they united to take on the foreign threat – international corporate laws and new institutions with real financial muscle to direct European industrial alliances into advanced sectors like space and computer-communications.

Initially, the nerve Servan Schreiber touched did not spark a new pan-European train of thought. But it did give added sense of purpose to existing national incentive schemes. In France, the ruling Gaullist conservatives were inspired to rework a traditional republican vision. Under this, the apparatus of the state would direct and assist private capital to establish the unique stamp of 'La France' in these industries.

This attempt was put into practice by merging the computer interests of three French electronics firms: their off-spring was named Compagnie Internationale pour L'Informatique (CII). The aim was to produce a French computer that could be sold against those produced by the US corporations, both in the domestic and world markets. This ambitious national strategy failed for two reasons. Firstly, the French computer company was unable to achieve economies of scale operating only in one country. Secondly, it lacked the necessary technical skills to be able to create a solely French-produced machine. There had to come a point when it must Europeanise its efforts.

Other European countries followed their own chosen paths. In England, a Labour government used the Industrial Re-Organisation Corporation as a marriage broker to form a single national computer company – ICL. In West Germany, the banks played the broker role with the state lurking supportively behind the scenes. Two corporations, AEG and Siemens, were allowed to compete in some areas and told to unite in others. But no matter how each nation did it, the aim was always the same: to try and create one or two organisations which would both bear the enormous research costs and be able to compete in the European and world markets dominated by US and Japanese corporations. (See background note 1.)

These corporations drew on national banks or government-supported investment agencies for their capital. They were also dependent on state telecommunications monopolies for the great bulk of their sales. This has created a peculiar situation in Europe. For in such a small geographic area there is an enormous number of incompatible telephone systems.

Crossed lines on the European exchange

The West Germans invested heavily in the world's first fully automatic direct dialling system in the 1950s, and the post and telephone monopoly, the Bundesposte, favoured national producers like Siemens with contracts. The agency also set equipment standards different enough from other national requirements that it was not cost efficient for foreign firms to run a special line just to serve the West German market. This 'widened the track' for national firms with access to loans and other state subsidies.

But once the Bundesposte had its system in place, contracts were thin on the ground. For almost a decade the West German telecommunications equipment market went slack. After 1980 the Bundesposte started planning various cable experiments, leading to replacement of copper cables by glass fibre cables. Yet these plans were small cheer to Siemens, which had never properly developed international markets and production facilities to the point where its fortunes plumetted after 1975.

In France, the telephone system was left to decay until 1975, when the decision was made on modernisation, beginning with an off-the-shelf digital-switching network. Through a form of import control called a 'market-entry-wall', only French-based companies won contracts. France now has one of the most advanced telephone and data switching systems in the world, but it has little in common with adjacent systems.

In Italy, on the other hand, the government has separated the national phone system from local companies. These local companies are left starved of cash and have been unable to modernise. To complicate things, three separate government ministries are responsible for three different parts of the system: local, national, and international.

During the last ten years the Italian government also did not have the money to modernise these systems. Today they are scrambling to buy new equipment. But it may be too little too late. Already private industry has seen the success of local television operating in defiance of the law, and it is preparing to do the same with data networks. So however it works out, Italy will soon have two or more competing telecommunications systems, each with its own de facto standards. On top of this each will be different from systems in other EEC nations.

There was a time when the encouragement of a national telecommunications industry could be seen as a positive step forward. Now it is holding back attempts to set a European standard which might enhance international competitiveness amongst the electronics corporations.

The EEC itself seems to have lost patience with the national post and telecommunications agencies. In 1981 EEC monopoly investigators accused the West German Bundesposte of being 'the worst offender', with its special standards and preferential contracts. The investigators told the EEC Commissioners that the Bundesposte's activities violated Article 85 of the Treaty of Rome (concerning restrictive practices). This charge is now a recurring theme amongst EEC diplomats and their advisers when they are proposing European computer-communications networks. (See background note 2.)

The interesting aspect to this problem is that there is really no longer a reason for these practices. Since 1975 most industry observers have admitted that purely national telecommunications industries were no longer feasible. Each of the very largest European corporations has already acknowledged the widening gap between themselves and the Americans or the Japanese, and they have rushed to make agreements for joint production with each other and with companies from one of the two foreign powers. (See background note 3.)

As a result, the European manufacturers of the 'new technologies' whether computer or telecommunications equipment, argue that they can go only two ways if they are to continue producing to compete with the Americans. Either they link up to create European-wide industrial alliances like Airbus Industrie, or they make a deal with the Japanese. In some cases it even pays to link up with one or two US firms. The object is to get the basic technologies in return for a share of the protected European market.

Eurocomputers: the French step out

In France, President Mitterand has seen this realisation as a neat way to socialise the economy. Renewing the Gaullist pledge to create a national electronics industry, the socialists invoked that fine old republican tradition by 'rationalising' the industry. At the end of 1981 the National Assembly passed legislation authorising nationalisation of the three largest electronics corporations – Compagnie General d'Electricite, Compagnie de Saint-Gobain (which owns CII-Honeywell-Bull and 30 per cent of the Italian giant Olivetti), and Thomson-Brandt. A fourth, Matra, would have a majority share allotted to the government.

The socialists also encouraged the renewal of technology licensing agreements for electronics components (particularly semi-conductors) with the US companies Honeywell, Tandy, Intel and National Semiconductor. Finally, the state has taken over direction of research, development and marketing activities for French electronics corporations both at home and abroad. The aim is to manage a major assault on world markets, challenging Japanese and American computer-communications systems with what the French call 'télématique'.

Although foreign firms have been grumbling, and some, like Honeywell, have sold off shares in their French holdings, no-one is going to leave. The French computer-communications market is the fastest growing in Europe, and Electronics firms will accept just about any rules in order to keep some presence. As Jacques Brunet, director of marketing for the American Intel company (which has a deal with Matra for production of semi-conductors) confided to Business Week magazine at the end of 1981: 'Once the dust settles, everyone has to get back to reality. The reality is that France is a big market.'

At certain points the French policy is similar to the long successful Japanese approach. In both countries the finance centres are closely aligned to the government: in Japan various ministries have had the final say on capitalisation; in France the banks have been nationalised.

In Japan the Ministry of International Trade and Industry (MITI) brought together top industrialists, worked out long-range goals and allotted 'tasks' to each corporation. The carrot was capital. The stick was MITI's power to grant import-export licences. In France managers and company directors have been spending an unprecedented amount of time listening to the women and men at the ministries. They are being 'guided' in their larger aims. The carrot is access to a large protected market, support for export initiatives and friendly relations with the banks. The stick is nationalisation. As a result, the French republican-socialist commitment to have the state throw the lead punch in the fight to conquer a portion of the world computer-communications market is now more intense than in any other EEC nation. (See background note 4.)

Most governments are content to continue providing schemes they hope will allow a national market base. Whether or not electronics companies are able and willing to move on to the international stage is a decision left to the company directors and their investors. This is a game with few players. Only firms with proven world markets, high levels of internally generated capital and a management structure which implements the 'American model' will get a stake. But three giants which have taken the plunge are Philips (Holland), Siemens (W. Germany) and Olivetti (Italy). Philips has taken the option of reorganisation to generate new technologies and markets without direct deals with foreign firms. With production for the European market representing 60 per cent of sales, factories have been closed and larger automated plants built to serve more than one country. A new holding company, Philips International, has been formed to manage all interests outside Holland, and 'new blood' has been brought in at the top from various foreign subsidiaries. The aim is to centralise marketing capabilities around a few high-technology products for sale in America and the Third World. Telecommunications equipment and videocassettes are two of the designated areas of emphasis, and for telecommunications the policy started paying off in 1981, when Philips landed 50 per cent of the largest contract for a phone system (Saudi Arabia) ever granted in the Third World.

The West German *Siemens* corporation, fifth largest electronics firm in the world, has remained one of the most 'home-bound' of all multinationals in computer-communications. An ageing management developed what some observers called a 'bunker mentality' throughout the 1960s and 1970s. There was also the fact that the special standards set by Germany's Bundesposte led to short production runs for hand-crafted equipment whilst the microelectronics innovations and automated assembly lines in Japan put the emphasis on functional design for mass produced components, often cheaper to replace than repair. By the time Siemens had designed one long-lasting component its competitors had moved through three product life-cycles, taking a profit each time.

By 1981 Siemens has to change its priorities. A new chief executive, Karlheinz Kaske, appointed 'efficiency-minded' managers who were told to cut marginal product lines and reorganise the whole corporate structure. 'We are spending almost ten per cent of sales on Research and Development', Kaske told Business Week in February, 1982. 'The German market is too small to provide the volume we need to support that level of spending.'

Kaske has put telecommunications at the centre of a new-look Siemens. The division has been told to concentrate on 'office-of-the-future' products while Kaske goes after preferential contracts from the Bundesposte and the EEC. To facilitate a quick entry into the market the company has also started making international deals. Fujitsu of Japan will provide IBM-compatible mainframe computers and Xerox of the United States will add its Ethernet local area network office machine connection system.

For its part, Siemens' world marketing team is pinning its hopes to a new digital PBX developed by the telecommunications division to handle 800 phone extensions. The United States is the main target. The 1981 corporate reorganisation meant Siemens' various US holdings were brought together under one American subsidiary, and with its new independence, more in line with American competitors, Siemens USA is hoping to capture ten per cent of the PBX market.

However, Siemens has kept one principle from the past. Foreign operations are built 'from the ground up' as extensions of the Bavarian organisation. It keeps the company peculiarly German in a trans-national electronics industry noted for the multinational composition of its employees.

Olivetti has used this latter technique to lead its growth across Europe and into international markets. After registering a 100 million dollar loss in 1978 a new chairman, Carlo De Benedetti, moved Americans into key management positions. Together with US trained Italians they reorganised along the 'three tier' American model, with emphasis on marketing for countries and regions.

A deal was made where Olivetti would sell Hitachi IBM-compatible mainframe computers and, De Benedetti went on a buying spree in the United States.

Olivetti purchased 11 US medium-sized hardware and software companies in 18 months from the autumn of 1978. A handful of typewriter and office machine companies were scooped up along the way, including Olympia and Logabax. De Benedetti also got a 'special' arrangement for penetration of the French market through Compagnie de Saint-Gobain, which owns 30 per cent of Olivetti. By the end of 1981 the newly international company was turning a profit and billing itself as the only European computer corporation capable of competing in world markets on a product for product basis with IBM.

To European socialists none of this is surprising. Corporations are a function of capitalism, and they can be expected to thrive under governments dedicated to managing capitalism. But what of the technologies themselves? The French Marxist communications analyst Armand Mattelart, for example, whilst noting the success of the European trade union group, the Fédération Européenne de la Metallurgie, in forcing Philips to accept the principle of trade union rights to information (a unique example) is still cynical about the communications technologies developed by such companies. In relation to the French government's experiment, Mattelart thunders rhetorically: 'Will these new technologies give democracy to those deprived of it? Will the softness of the information overcome the barriers between nations, groups, classes and castes?'

Mattelart thinks not. 'At the moment, these innovations accompany corruption, accentuate social disparities and reinforce doctrines of national security,' he writes: Mattelart believes that the corporate doctrine is as pungent as the products. Unlike their American counterparts, more prompt and pragmatic, who don't allow themselves to consider the social and cultural stakes in this technological leap, French telecommunications exporters present in their discussions models of the restructuring of society through technology. Trying to use these corporations as the vehicle for change by pandering 'sinister' economic interests behind a techno-humanist smoke-screen is a recipe for disaster, say the French Marxists.

Mitterand's ministers still think it's a viable risk, as long as most of the corporations are nationalised. Industry Minister Pierre Dreyfus, with three of the largest now under his control, has complete faith that the corporations will do for the state what they have not done for themselves. 'My greatest concern is that the nationalisation results in dynamic companies', he told journalists after the National Assembly gave its stamp of approval. 'It is the most appropriate way to enable French industry to meet the international challenge which has placed it in difficulty.'

Whether nationalising corporations with the same staff, products, techniques, and concepts laid down in 'the American model' will allow France to make something different of computer-communications remains to be seen. What can be said is that there are now two formulae for the introduction of computer-communications technologies at work in Europe. Both accept the American corporate model as the de facto standard form, and both believe a single nation can no longer provide a launching pad for success – measured by innovation, employment, market penetration and profitability. But one further believes that a merged and sheltered private sector is best placed to introduce the technology and a notion of how to use it. Dreyfus believes that an aggressive public sector fired by nationalism and well schooled in corporate methodology can profitably deliver a unique variation of this new technological form, complete with instructions for social change.

Eurotelevision: the underground of the air

The two social workers from Utrecht and their artist friend from Amsterdam were enjoying a sunny day on the beach. 'What's new? Well there's cable television. Just about everybody has it,' said one of the social workers. 'But what's intimidating about that is you almost have no choice. The government more or less makes it mandatory. I think for me its coming down to a matter of my own individual rights whether I have a cable in the house or not.'

70

> '*That might be so*', argued the Amsterdam artist, '*but the potential is superb. You never know what is going to turn up on that television after the regularly relayed stations shut down. The cable companies don't close off their signal, so pirates have been beaming illegal signals towards the cable companies' antennae. The programmes go right onto the cable and appear in your home on some channel which carries a foreign signal that shuts down early.*'
>
> '*Some of it is very commercial – American movies with lots of local advertising. But every once in a while there is something very underground, if you know what I mean. I reserve judgement.*'
>
> '*That's all very well for you in Amsterdam,*' responded the social worker, '*but for us in Utrecht it's nothing but commercial television. If that's cable television they can keep it. My daughter is already polluted enough by the programmes we get now.*'

In the summer of 1982 this conversation could have happened almost anywhere in Western Europe. Television is on the verge of a major shake-up.

European television systems emerged originally as the jealously guarded prerogative of the state. For the most part this remains the case. There may be structures which aim to assure the democratic control of the media, as in Holland and West Germany, but these have not noticeably affected the kinds of programmes they produce. The principle of state control for political reasons has been reworked in each country and sold to the public as firstly, necessary to protect and encourage a unique cultural identity, and secondly, to protect and encourage a national media industry. For the last seven years, however, broadcasting monopolies have had stiff competition, and there are now signs that the audience will no longer buy the monopoly principle.

In France, a socialist victory at the 1981 elections unleashed a feverish spread of 'underground' broadcasting. Radio stations led the way. They proliferated to the extent that President Mitterand had no choice but to legalise them, just so they could be properly monitored, although he also took the precaution of banning advertising. There have been fewer underground television stations in France, but their political effect is, in some ways, more significant.

> *On a September day in 1981 Jean-Baptiste Piazzano and Claude Jaget put the final touches to a transmitter on the roof of a house in the suburbs of Lyon. They then climbed down to the studio and turned on Channel 22, France's first 'free' television station. 'With a little more money we'll be able to reach the whole city', says Piazzano. 'If we get that, and government approval, we can go on to a full schedule in the New Year. Our case is before the Prime Minister himself at this very moment.'*

Piazzano, and his committee of ten fellow libertarian socialists, are out to put the case for alternative media structures into practice. They will broadcast programmes of 'information, entertainment, original creative productions and special services open to the community,' and they intend to stay free of any special interest groups, 'whether they be financial, political or from the world of advertising.'

Channel 22 and its many sister radio stations are the latest outpouring from a well-developed alternative media movement, which has been organising itself since the mid-1960s. In their manifesto they reject the present form of 'telematique' as the cutting edge of American economic domination. Worse, they see the one-way flow inherent in this system as a new weapon deployed by the forces of authority and hierarchy against ordinary people, who would otherwise spontaneously construct their own information and culture through democratic association.

Under the guise of public service, they argue, this system sets out to create markets for already existing corporate forms which have shown themselves to be only interested in the maximisation of profit. Within the logic of this system, people exist in their homes to work for the corporations. Their functions are closely monitored and catalogued, and the contents of the information-entertainment files are filled with material according to the most basic notions of behaviourist psychology. The fact that a single screenpage or short 'print-out' contains only a small piece of the whole picture also contributes to the formation of frustration. That frustration will bring the consumer back to the screen over and over again. Every time the screen is consulted the person must pay.

It is on these same grounds that cable television and Pay-TV are rejected. In their place 'Tele Libre' proposes an alternative media system built around Citizens Band Radio (CB), and truely local radio and television.

'CB', states the manifesto, 'by being a two-way democratic system, can create a new sort of solidarity, it can re-launch a telecommunications industry less alienating than the télématique gadgets. Free radio stations must be allowed to flourish in response to any and all groups within society who wish to be in touch with their own information and cultural objectives. There should be one rule: no advertising. There should be one constraint: the content and structure of all broadcasts should be erected in respect of the 'space' of others. Truely local radio and television should be allowed to flourish, not media of 'consensus', nor of special regulating agencies, nor under 'municipal' control, local TV and radio must be seen as a public resource which may be used by each community brought together in democratic exchange of all opinions.'

These principles have gained support among all political groupings to the left of Mitterrand except the Communist party, which is suspicious of their libertarian and radical 'culturalists' proponents. Prime target among Communists is the Paris daily Liberation. The paper has reported each 'underground' advance with positive relish. Alternative policies and scenarios, particularly for community cable television and local control of programmes broadcast by satellite, have been given much space for detailed argument.

Many of President Mitterrand's computer-communications advisers equally share this critique of télématique. But the massive public and private commitment to the new computer-communications has kept them silent. The 'establishment' of research, administration and the electronics industry built up around this new white hope has told the President that any deviation from this modernising path would seriously wound 'La Patrie'. Overseas markets and French world cultural influence might dwindle. Unemployment would surely rise. The door would be opened even wider to American domination, followed quickly by aggressive Japanese corporations.

France, seeming to be out of step with the rest of the world, could also fall behind in educational development. The people of France would see others enjoying the benefits of computer-communications and hate the President for refusing to let them have them. At the EEC, other nations will once again condemn France for making its own priorities the stumbling block to united action in spheres related to computer-communications.

All this is set against a totally alternative media proposal from Mitterrand's own movement. This system, say its proponents, is the only one which can provide the very decentralisation and democratisation on which his party counts so much for re-educating the people of France away from their neo-conservative past.

For the moment there is a compromise: existing télématique development programmes remain in place; a new government-inspired shuffle of electronics firms is in motion to search, once more, for a truly national computer industry; and the broadcasting system has been put at one remove from Presidential control. So reforms are taking place, though hardly shifting the balance towards the alternative. Instead, they have given a socialist-humanist tinge to television, a libertarian glow around radio and a gleam in the eyes of satellite TV backers. (See background note 5.)

For the next few years the French socialist government will undoubtedly walk a narrow line between its own party and the computer-communications establishment. But whether or not télématique is a success, the modest path charted for broadcasting in France already makes that country stand out against the current European trend towards commercialisation and Americanisation.

Eurotelevision: satellites cast their (American) shadow

Italian broadcasting has already entered a new age of privitisation. Local commercial television stations used the courts to pry open a state monopoly in 1976. By 1982, commercial networks were feeding some 400 stations a steady diet of Hollywood telefilms. One network hopes to begin competing with the state network (RAI) in 1983, with a news programme based on the CBS network in the United States.

In Holland, a television system considered to be one of the most democratic in the world is reeling from a series of political dislocations and commercial intrusions led by pirate cable TV. Dutch television critics now speak of the 'inevitable introduction of commercial programming'.

Similar comments can be heard in most European nations, and the cause is seen as the imminent arrival of Direct Broadcasting from Satellite (DBS), bringing with it a flood of American programmes and consumer advertising. Luxembourg and Monaco, for example, have given notice they will be broadcasting French and Italian programmes from satellites before the end of the decade. France and Italy have accepted this commercial 'fait accompli' by taking shares in Tele Monte Carlo's satellite channel company.

Commercial DBS advocates say there is no evidence to show that satellite television would homogenise content and lower the tone of national services. But some Europeans have already had a chance to judge for themselves. Since April 1982 any cable operator with a three metre diameter dish aerial and a government permit has been able to relay Europe's first commercial satellite channel.

Based in London, Satellite Television rents space on the European Space Agency's Orbital Test Satellite (OTS), which has a 'footprint' stretching from Tunisia to Helsinki and from mid-Spain to the Western edge of the Soviet Union. By August 1982 Satellite Television was providing a nightly two hours of programmes with up to seven minutes of advertising per hour. A quarter of a million people were watching these programmes in Scandinavia and Switzerland, where 70% of all televisions are attached to cables. Test services were in operation for West Germany, France, Austria and Denmark.

According to a company press release, a typical evening's programme schedule might include soccer, five year old British situation comedies, Hollywood movies, documentaries in the style of National Geographic/ Time-Life, American rock music or telefilms like 'Charlie's Angels'. Speaking at the 1982 Edinburgh International Television Festival, Brian Haynes, Director of Satellite Television emphasised that a satellite company was not responsible for such content. 'Satellite Television is simply the carrier. The complementarities between satellities and cables means that people do not watch satellites and cables. People watch programmes. The programme makers are the ones affecting the audience. They make the products.' But besides glossing over the role it plays by selecting already-made British and US programmes, Satellite Television often forgets to say it pays for its 'product' by selling commercials. The advertising industry is well aware of the potential.

Jim Shaw, marketing manager of the London commercial station Thames Television, asked a series of telling questions at that same Edinburgh Conference: 'Just how wide will you spread your marketing net when your commercial, possibly quite by accident, maybe even out of your control, will cover most of Europe? Will you opt for national or Euro brands. And which country will you choose for a test market?' A number of large corporations are in fact already at work to smooth out potential marketing problems caused by separate national agencies, products and images. Cadbury-Schweppes, says Shaw, is typical: 'Their international marketing department is working to a common theme that will work for them in every one of the 150 countries in which they market their products.'

There are also other developments in the air. Nearly all the televisions in the Benelux countries are already cabled. West German and French government communications ministers speak of 'scrambled signal subscription television'. The Italian government plans to take part in European Space Agency television programme exchanges and launch its own DBS satellite towards the end of the decade. By that time the private Italo-American networks will dwarf the state system by a ratio of two to one.

As one French observer to the Edinburgh International Television Festival put it: 'That there will be cable and satellite broadcasting is now taken for granted. Most advocates say they can only be made economic by being commercial or collecting subscriptions. Either way the commercial ethic will drive the operator to find his product at the cheapest possible price. The bargain basement of world television is in Hollywood and America.'

The French, meanwhile, are travelling their separate road. Stipulations attached to the 1981 Communications Act (passed by the socialist National Assembly) restrict the importation of American programmes, ensure special levies to finance French production and mark a preference for Third World telefilms when buying foreign programmes. There is no expectation that commercial DBS will be allowed to reach French television during President Mitterrand's term of office.

But Mitterrand is treading a solitary path with these policies. Early in 1981, during an official visit to Italy, the President urged Italian politicians to limit the incursion of American broadcasting patterns. He called for talks to sponsor Franco-Italian productions. The Italians, uncharacteristically, listened but did not respond.

Background notes

Background note 1
The National Imperative

Electronics corporations did not merge across Europe. Instead, they moved from a national base to compete, in the first instance, for other national markets, and then (when possible) moved production across national borders. Each country has promoted national corporations in a different way, the result of a process better called 'concentration' than merger. The effect has been the same. Here are four examples:

France
Mergers took off in France after 1968. In that year the government assisted at 2,200 corporate marriages. The next year 1,800 took place. In 1970 the government formed the Institut de Dévelopment Industriel (IDI) with a budget of one billion francs and a mandate to encourage French firms to form bigger units and compete internationally.

Amongst electronics firms, Thomson-CSF and CGE were together allowed to pick up 45 per cent of all electronics sales revenues through acquisition of small firms. The two had also just completed their own merger-acquisition process: a new company, Compagnie Internationale pour l'Informatique (CII) was formed, with government incentive, and brought together the data processing interests of Thomson, CGE and a third, smaller company Schneider. Under the 'Plan Calcul', CII was given state capital and preferential contracts. It managed to originate a French computer (Iris). But IBM still maintained its market dominance. IDI then pushed both companies to move into foreign markets. CGE was predominantly a French company, but with government support it produced a five-year plan which would make foreign sales 55 per cent of production by 1977. Thomson-CSF had a head start. By 1974, 48 per cent of sales revenue came from subsidiaries, and in 1975 a new company, Thomson-CSF International, was running an armaments factory in Germany, a rural telephone producer in Argentina, a major radio equipment and electronics components factory in Morocco and similar factories in Brazil and Spain.

West Germany
Germany fosters a close three-cornered relationship between government, banks and corporations. The government likes to see the semblance of competition maintained by having more than one national conglomerate in each sector. The banks make this possible by offering many more specialist services than in other nations. Three banks – Deutsche Bank, Dresdener Bank and Commerzbank – are the glue of the economy. They lend to the corporations which, in other nations, would raise money through the stock market; they play the stock market for themselves and their customers; they act as stockbrokers offering new share issues; and they take a specific interest in the development of businesses. As a result, bank directors are found on the boards of most of West Germany's corporations. In fact they hold so many cross-industry board positions that a law had to be passed in the 1960s to limit the number of board memberships per bank director to ten.

West Germany has fostered two corporations in the electronics and telecommunications sector: AEG-Telefunken and Siemens. Through their shared directorships, and the interest of the government in conquering new markets, these companies embarked on a joint drive throughout the 1970s. The conglomerates formed two subsidiaries, for example: Kraftwerk Union (power generating equipment) and Transformatoren Union (sodium-cooled fast breeder reactors).

From then on, however, they followed different strategies. Siemens went for total centralisation of all aspects of its vast electronics interests on its headquarters in Munich. AEG, West Germany's ninth largest manufacturing company, had lost more than 60 per cent of its assets to East Germany after partition. It had to borrow heavily and buy as many small electronics companies as it could to continue to be competitive. This meant it was diversified (without the benefit of highly developed information-handling capabilities) and continuously in debt.

Italy
Mussolini knew that Italy needed a strong national financial organism capable of generating funding and management superstructure to compete for new industrial markets. He formed the Istituto per la Ricostruzione Industriale. By the 1960s this quasi-government finance and investment organisation owned 140 companies in telecommunications, broadcasting, banking, steel and associated manufacturing industries. These companies also acted as 'handmaidens' to the vast private commercial empires like Fiat and Olivetti.

Holland
Holland means Philips, the fourth largest electronics firm in the world. Its own post-war expansion was steady and unencumbered by the need to rely on special state assistance. In 1959 it had a turnover of 1.3 billion dollars; by 1974 this had grown to ten billion dollars.

Philips is not a European company. It has established its position by expanding from Holland into the Third World, where wage levels make manufacturing particularly cost-effective and profitable. In 1974 it had factories in 40 countries and sales in 60.

'Fourteen years after the creation of the Common Market, Philips, in spite of geographical dispersion, did not yet exploit the advantages of economies of scale. The firm was still traditionally organised so as to extract the largest profit from each national market on the basis of a network of factories set up in each, producing for local consumption.' (Armand Mattelart, *Multinational Corporations and the Control of Culture*, Harvester Press, 1979)

Background note 2
EEC Projects for All-Europe Computer-Communications

Data Networks

In the late 1970s the EEC Commission's Directorate for Scientific and Technical Information brought together a consortium of member states' post and telephone agencies to construct Euromet. This is an international data network carrying scientific and technical information. The consortium is called Direct Information Access Network for Europe (DIANE). The service went into operation during 1980, and by the spring of 1982 it had 1,500 users making 20,000 calls a month to 25 'host' computers, in turn providing access to 223 databases. The EEC has also inaugurated a scheme to provide 'incentive funds' so that more private databases can be brought into this public network.

The EEC Commissioners consider the project a success. An 'information market' has been created which is currently forecast to grow at a rate of between 20 and 35 per cent a year. The United Kingdom, France, West Germany and Italy account for 65 per cent of the data communication in the Community.

Most of the computer hardware involved comes from International Computers Ltd (UK) and Siemens (West Germany). The blossoming market has also been joined by private networks: Transpac (a consortium of French electronics firms), Telenet and Tymenet of the United States (giving access to North American data bases) and the international financial exchange network SWIFT. At the end of 1981 the EEC announced its intention to 'privatise' Euronet by slowly divesting itself of its 50 per cent stake.

The Commissioners are now embarking on a new project called the Inter-Institutional Integrated Services Information System (INSIS). This will be a shared private network linking various member government ministries, EEC offices and affiliated institutions. This is seen as an incentive for the establishment of European networking standards, and an encouragement to national post/telephone agencies and electronics industries to develop pan-European equipment designs competitive with Japanese and American machinery.

Satellites

In 1974 the EEC brought together the European Space Research Organisation and the European Launcher Development Organisation to form the European Space Agency (ESA). Its stated purpose was to initiate large scale co-operative space projects amongst the Ten, which might provide electronics and space companies with contracts to develop capabilities in areas where US corporations were dominant.

Existing and future programmes include:

The Orbital Test Satellite (1978). An experimental satellite which offered capacity for 3,000 telephone circuits and two TV channels. It has served as the basis for the design of:

The European Communications Satellites. A series of five satellites will be built by a ten-nation consortium of companies, led by the British Aerospace Dynamics Group. ECS1 was launched in the spring of 1982, ECS2 is scheduled for 1983. The other three will be used as spares so that the system can continue to perform through the 1990s in line with a contract between the European Space Agency and ECS's operating consortium, Eutelsat (a link-up between European telecommunications organisations). Eutelsat will use the satellites to complement telecommunications services in each member nation, to exchange TV programmes between members of the European Broadcasting Union, to carry data transmissions, and to allow communication with offshore oil and gas rigs.

Maritime Communications Satellites. With major UK funding and contracts, these are two satellites designed to increase efficiency of ship-to-shore communications. Marec A is now operating over the Atlantic. Marec B will operate over the Pacific.

78

The Large-scale Communications Satellite. This is a showpiece project. It is planned as a multi-purpose space platform capable of extensive broadcasting services. Prime contractor is British Aerospace. Launch is set for 1986.

All these satellites and others, many from the Third World and some from the United States, are launched on Arianne rockets. The Arianne was developed by the European Space Agency, but is now a private company, Ariannespace. Shareholders include 36 European space components manufacturers, 11 banks and the French Centre d'Études Spatiales (CNES), which has 34 per cent of the shares.

Background note 3
West Germany: Siemens

Siemens, amongst the five largest electronics and telecommunications equipment firms in the world, is highly centralised and vertically integrated. It has grown slowly through the principle of building up its own products and markets rather than merger or acquisition. However, as the 1970s wore on, this tactic started to lose the company a great deal of money: IBM and ITT took away its European markets and IBM in particular maintained a steady 60 per cent of Siemens' home market. The only way the company maintained a coherent market share was through support from the government. To reverse the trend towards increased losses in the computer field, the following moves were made:

Late 1960s:
Co-operative agreement with RCA (USA) for mainframe computer architecture and software. Siemens' computers constructed around this agreement, machines sold mainly in West Germany.

1971:
RCA pulls out of the computer business with little consultation with Siemens. The German company left with a line of 'hollow' products, and enters into agreement with Philips (Netherlands) and Cii (France) to develop Unidata, a European computer manufacturer.

The Netherlands: Philips

Philips is the largest private employer in Europe. After an initial failure to see how American multinationals were using the pan-European market, Philips has attempted to move away from being a family firm into separate production and marketing organisations in each country where it operates, with American-style rationalisation.

In 1971 Philips joined Siemens (West Germany) and Cii (France) in the computer company Unidata. By 1973 the company had failed and Philips had withdrawn to lick its wounds. There would be no more collaborations unless Philips had total control, and strategies emerged to make the corporation itself capable of regenerating itself through internal reorganisation.

'In the new era, under the sign of North American management, the number of factories making radio sets was reduced from 14 to nine, the number making turntables from eight to three. Each was produced for the entire company and not only for the national market. Production of cheap tape recorders was centralised in two factories in Austria and Belgium; the Netherlands now provides electric shavers . . . washing machines come from Britain, Italy and France. Dishwashers are made in Germany. . . European production provides the company with the largest part of its production turnover (69 per cent in 1974).' (Armand Mattelart, *Multinational Corporations and the Control of Culture*, Harvester Press, 1979, page 25)

At the end of the 1970s, however, Philips saw that this tactic had not worked. It was not generating large enough profits from its European operation, and it was losing out to Japanese companies in the consumer electronics sector. By 1980 profits had dropped 42 per cent in a year to about 100 million dollars. The problem, said the company's new president Wisse Dekker, was its 'family' structure and dependency on the EEC consumer electronics market.

For Philips, telecommunications equipment was the big money spinner. With a large slice of the fibre optics, micro-chip and data-processing market in this sector, years of R&D have been paying off in big contracts, like one shared with the Swedish firm L. M. Ericsson for the installation of the Saudi Arabian telephone system. It was the Europe-wide consumer and computer electronics sector where the company had been failing, and even where it had innovated a new product, like the video cassette recorder, JVC (Victor company of Japan) had been able to undersell it.

Action was taken after 1980. The Dutch management base was widened once more. Wisse Dekker himself came from outside the inner sanctum, historically close to the family, and had received his training during years managing Philips operations in Japan, Indonesia and Britain. A new holding company, Philips International, was formed, of which the Philips company of Holland would be just one part, no longer able to call the shots for the world operation.

Philips employed 370,000 people, 62 per cent outside Holland, and the new rationalisation plan called for a loss of 20,000 jobs across Europe, with a series of factory closures. These included a data systems plant in Rotterdam as well as facilities in Germany, Finland, Britain, Spain, Belgium, Italy, France and Switzerland. This would pressage a further centralisation of production for colour TV tubes, audio equipment, lamps and electronics components (micro-chips, etc.), and capacity would be found in newly automated factories. One example is a 150 million dollar video recorder facility at Vienna, where computer-controlled robots assemble 750,000 recorders a year assisted by 2,000 employees. Other assembly tasks are to be moved to Asia and Latin America.

Meanwhile, Philips will centre introduction of new products on the United States. Its marketing departments have decided that the European-wide market is simply not capable of taking to innovations quickly enough to make the research and development costs pay off.

Background note 4
Mitterrand's Grand Plan

Within a year of taking office the French Socialist government had delivered an integrated plan for the organisation of a national computer-communications offensive. The plan is designed to create 'industrial socialism' by guiding the integration and development of four sectors: chemicals, electronics, health and associated materials. The policy aims to modernise lagging industries (like steel and textiles), link research with production at all levels, and create jobs. The sector which will lead this plan is electronics. The hope is to make France the third technological power after the United States and Japan.

To allow this 'national guidance' to occur in the electronics industry the government has embarked on a 'rationalisation' programme to limit competition and to position companies to take on foreign competition. Discussions have been underway to nationalise the interests of ITT, to merge the two largest telecommunications equipment manufacturers (CIT-Alcatel and Thomson-Brandt), to take control of the designated computer-components manufacturer Cii-Honeywell-Bull, and to force agreements between these and other companies in France and abroad which might bring new technologies under French control.

Altogether, 150 million dollars has been allocated to a five-year plan for the electronics sector. Ninety million dollars will go for research and development. Sixty million dollars will come in loans to capitalise the microelectronics components manufacturers. The Ministry of Research and Technology, which oversees most of the nation's research, was given 3 billion dollars to spend in 1982. This is how some of the money will be spent:

1. The Museum of Science and Technology will sponsor a programme of research leading to a 1985 national conference on France's place in 'high technology'.

2. A new research centre will be set up called the Study Centre for Advanced Systems and Technologies (CESTA). The centre will bring together researchers and industrialists to develop plans for new products and processes in terms of 'networks'.

3. The World Centre for Microcomputers, whose chairman is Jean-Jacques Servan Schreiber. It is an international laboratory for the development of microcomputers, and there are hopes that affiliated laboratories will emerge in Canada, the United States, Japan, the OPEC nations and the Third World. The annual budget is 20 million dollars. There are 'open' offices in Paris where anyone can come off the street and play with micros. The laboratory will work to develop new 'humanistic' languages for the micro, show how the machine can be used to retrain workers displaced through automation, and apply the benefits of micro systems to the needs of people in the rural Third World.

Background note 5
European Television at the Crossroads

France

In 1974 the French state television organisation ORTF was reorganised. At the time, President Giscard d'Estaing was under considerable pressure to put broadcasting into private hands. He refused, saying that he could not risk losing control of an essential political instrument'. Instead, ORTF became three television channels, one providing regional programmes. At the same time, three foreign television stations, all commercial, have large audiences in France: Tele Luxembourg, Tele Belge (two programmes in French) and Tele Monte Carlo.

France has a limited number of experimental cable systems. These were set up after 1972 in seven cities. There is also a fibre optics experiment in Biarritz, and the French PTT has a viewdata cable experiment in Brittany, though this does not offer traditional cable television programming.

The future application of a cable TV system was graphically illustrated for the inhabitants of Metz when the system was used to rebroadcast foreign programmes as well as the three national channels. Many thought the whole thing superfluous; 'more of the same' was the comment of one journalist. The experiment is now in abeyance while France debates the whole media framework.

There is a lot to consider. In addition to the experimental cables there are a few small systems in areas where standard aerial reception of the national channels is impossible. The main cable technology companies say these are enough to provide the germ for a national system to carry interactive information services and to deliver a proposed national satellite TV channel. These companies are Thomson, Philips and CGE (through its subsidiary Cable de Lyons).

Another proposal before the government is to transmit the proposed satellite programmes on a second 819-line channel (like the existing main ORTF station). West Germany and France are also talking about satellite co-operation, France is buying into Tele Monte Carlo's proposed satellite station, and the European Commission has a number of proposals it would like to interest the French in.

Since his ascendancy President Mitterrand has in fact been treading a narrow path between the commercial interests already in place and the proposals for an alternative media system coming from within his own left-wing coalition. But first on the agenda has been a reform of the existing television system. This has always been the poor sister of French media and the arts, seen by intellectuals as 'bread and circuses' directed from the offices of President and Prime Minister. The exception has been news and public affairs, where a few journalists have fought political pressures to put French documentation among the world's best.

The Socialists have decided that television should respond to the new national political culture in parallel to other institutions catching a breeze from the bourgeois left. This is the story so far:

1. Soon after the 1981 election a subtle purge occurred throughout the industry. Administrators and programme-makers seen as instruments of neo-conservative ideology were told that their positions might become untenable. Many resigned.

2. A Ministry of Communications was formed to take over the Prime Minister's traditional responsibility for broadcasting. Prime Minister Pierre Mauroy also set up a Commission of Enquiry into broadcasting headed by Pierre Moinot. The Moinot Commission reported in September 1981.

3. In April 1982 an Audio-Visual Bill was laid before the National Assembly. It incorporated most of the recommendations of the Moinot Commission. There were three principles: decentralisation, autonomy and creativity.
(a) Decentralisation: FR3 would be made a truly regional television system. In addition to existing

82

television stations in Lyons, Lille and Marseilles, new stations would be built in Rennes, Bordeaux, Toulouse, Strasbourg, Corsica and Paris. In time, FR3 would be replaced by a national association of regional television companies administered by 22 regional communications councils, with representatives from the press, advertising, politicians and the general public. The association will be empowered to arrange finance and networking of programmes drawn from local production companies.
(b) Autonomy: The state would maintain a monopoly of broadcasting as a 'public service' and a new authority would oversee all its activities. The state would continue financing the television system and advertising would be held at 25 per cent of revenue provision. There will be no national commercial television system and community-based local 'free' stations would not be allowed for the time being.
(c) Creativity: The two national channels (TF1 and Antenne 2) can no longer compete with each other for ratings. They have to complement each other, particularly with services for minorities. More money will be available for co-production of French programmes for the two channels. A new company has also been formed to market French programmes in foreign markets.
The number of films shown on television will be reduced, and their cost to channels will include a surcharge designed to cover production costs. The quota limits for American programmes will be severely reduced. When foreign programmes are purchased, productions from the Third World will be given preference.

4. In August 1982 the state broadcasting apparatus was placed under the control of an independent 'Haute Autorité'. The board has nine members and a 'president' with a casting vote. Three members are appointed by the President, three by the president of the National Assembly, and three by the president of the Senate. One-third of these appointees will be replaced every three years. The first president of this Haute Autorité is a socialist journalist, Michel Cotta.

Italy

Television came under the control of the state agency Radiotelevisione Italien – Societa per Aziono (RAI) at its inception in 1954. By 1970 the company had three channels, and is said to have reached saturation when the number of television receivers passed the ten million mark in 1971. RAI carries advertising 'bunched' in five-minute slots between programmes.

RAI's monopoly was effectively broken in 1972 when Parliamentary deadlock caused its legal mandate to lapse. Local social, political and advertising groups took the opportunity to set up a series of independent stations and small cable systems. They thrived by providing rebroadcasts of foreign signals, mainly from Tele Monte Carlo, Lugano in Switzerland and Capodistria in Yugoslavia.

This groundswell came at a particularly portentous political moment. Sectarianism was peaking as the Catholic Church and the ruling Christian Democratic party were falling to defeat in their attempt to win a referendum designed to revoke legislation allowing divorce. The whole upsurge was accompanied by predictions of a new libertarian media age centred on cable television. This didn't happen. After an initial turn under the spotlight of public interest, the technical complications of actually cabling-up the nation overcame the small-capital interests involved.

Local television stations were more successful. They provided cheap American programmes and rebroadcasts from cross-border stations. At first they were tracked down and closed by officials from the PTT. But a series of court battles culminated in 1976 when local stations won the right to keep broadcasting.

Today, commercial networks serve the local stations. The law still forbids transmission of private networks nationally, but the private networks have got round this proviso by pre-recording blocks of programmes days in advance, copying them on to videocassettes, and delivering them by hand to local stations which 'just happen' to play the programme blocks simultaneously.

There are currently 400 private stations in Italy. In 1980 numbers peaked at 500. Then, accelerating costs forced many smaller units out of business. About 100 stations are connected to the three main networks – Canale 5, Rete 4 and Italia Uno. These are growing by leaps and bounds, whilst stations started as community-interest programmes are falling by the wayside. Those who try to go the commercial route independently find they are undercut by the networks.

There is little doubt about what these networks are selling to the Italian people. As one Italian official put it: 'Last year (1981) the commercial networks bought 100 million dollars worth of American programmes. Italy is now second only to Britain as the importer of American programmes'. In March 1982 one American TV executive told the *International Herald Tribune*: 'In the last two years they bought up the whole Hollywood backlog, everything left on the shelves since the end of the war, including black-and-white films and even silent footage.'

With Italy now boasting more telvision stations *per capita* than any other nation on earth, mostly served with American programmes, there is a resigned acceptance amongst non-commercial broadcasters that the future belongs to those who provide an ever-voracious audience with more American made sponsored entertainment. Some even welcome the development, saying it will cause RAI to shake off some of the deadwood inhabiting its programming departments.

RAI has one final ace up its sleeve. It is the only television facility allowed, by law, to broadcast news. The commercial networks are campaigning hard to gain this right at the same time as they hope to be allowed to distribute their programmes via terrestrial microwave towers. Again there is a difference of opinion over how the commercial networks might treat the news. The RAI news programmes now have the largest single audience of any television

programme; but many say this is simply because the audience has no choice. Broadcasters at the nation's second largest commercial network, Canale 5, are quite prepared to say that their model for broadcasting is CBS in the United States (CBS), and they hope to be able to provide news programmes in similar style.

The Italian government has no plans for its own television satellite. It has taken a 25 per cent share in one of the European Space Agency projects for a large-scale communications satellite (L-Sat), planned for operation after 1986. But there is reason to believe that smaller European nations will beam Italian programmes at the nation, and there is no reason why these will not be picked up and rebroadcast by local stations or the networks. To cover its bets, the Italian government has taken up an option on 60 per cent of the equity for a proposed commercial satellite television station in Monte Carlo. 'No matter what happens,' said one Italian TV producer, 'we are now in an advertising-based television society. I do not see this changing. I do see RAI shrinking. American culture has conquered Italian media.'

The Netherlands

There are two television stations in the Netherlands. Each one is served by a group of programme-making associations alloted time according to the number of subscribers they have. The broadcasting companies are:

NOS:
The state co-ordinating broadcasting company. It is given 25 per cent of the time available for TV transmission. In addition it operates transmitter facilities and pays for an orchestra and other cultural facilities which can be shared amongst the other broadcasting groups. It is the co-operating agency for Eurovision and other all-Europe TV activities.
AVRO:
Conservative broadcasting union started as a radio broadcasting company in 1923.
TROS:
Neutral to right of centre politically, this is a relatively new addition to the group. According to one Dutch TV analyst: 'It does everything but play

84

commercials. It provides the mother-lode of popular cultural schmaltz accompanied by an aggressive, levelling right-wing presentation of news and commentary. It panders to the worst emotions in Dutch people and is thought responsible for growing right-wing thinking and racism.'

KRO (Catholic):
Broadcasting association run by the notoriously liberal Dutch Catholic Church. It has a reputation for presenting some of the most searching news and documentary programmes made in Europe. In 1982 Holland was outraged when four TV journalists working for KRO were gunned down in El Salvador while trying to make a programme.

NCRV (Protestant):
Closely aligned with the mainstream of Protestant-Christian social mores in the country. Usually more conservative than KRO, it has been the last of the large organisations to allow unedited cultural programming.

VARA (Socialist):
Consistently the most aggressive politically. Its continuous hammering at social and political imbalances in Holland and abroad throughout the 1960s is credited with bringing large numbers towards the Labour Party.

VPRO (Christian non-conformist):
Popular amongst the socially-conscious middle classes (social workers, teachers, etc.), this is one of the smaller organisations, and did not get a chance to mount a coherent schedule of programmes until a second TV channel was opened up.

EO (right-wing fundamentalist):
Unashamedly conservative Protestant organisation. Small, but vocal, it appeals to the rural regions and has a consistent following. It shows American programmes when it is not broadcasting religious programmes. 'Every organisation must provide several hours of documentaries and other general programmes,' says the Utrecht analyst. 'To give you an example of how this is accomplished by EO, they would make a programme to show that the theories of evolution are bankrupt. This is Christian broadcasting.'

VOO (neutral):
'This station grew out of Radio Veronica, a pirate rock music station of the 1960s. Its programmes lean towards that style but because they cannot have many hours (they have less than 100,000 subscribers) what emerges is a mish-mash of programming like Britain's "Top Of The Pops" or "Solid Gold" from the United States'.

Cable TV

Nearly 80 per cent of the Netherlands is cabled. Only the rural areas in the North and East of the country are largely without cable. The PTT, in association with local private companies – common carriers with little or no control over programming – has been developing the service, and the government hopes to have the whole country cabled by 1984. Observers predict 1987 as a more likely date.

Viewers who have cable can receive these services: two Dutch channels; three German channels; four Belgian channels (two in French, two in Dutch). Recently, one of the Belgian stations has started joint productions with the Dutch television system: this happened during the 1981 World Cup broadcasts. In some parts of the country it is possible to receive other national services, either by cable or by aerial. For example, in The Hague cable systems offer two British services – ITV (Anglia) and BBC1. In the North (Friesland) it is possible to receive one or both of the Danish TV services. Sub-titles are provided for translation.

Pirate Television Stations

Cable operators have tended to leave the whole system 'open' until all the stations they are rebroadcasting have stopped transmitting. Some stations stop earlier than others. Around 1980 a number of enterprising TV pirates therefore started beaming signals at the receiving aerials of the cable systems. Viewers would receive programmes on the 'open' channels. In the first instance the channel reserved for one of the German stations was used, then one of the channels used for a Belgian/French service was added.

These cable 'pirates' broadcast mostly movies, usually under three years old. They paid no copyright and put on commercials in between. Their main focus of operation was Amsterdam. but a few have been set up throughout the Randstadt, the central region of the Netherlands, taking in Amsterdam, Rotterdam, The Hague and Utrecht. When this happened the companies owning copyright on the programmes got together with film theatre owners to prosecute the pirates. They also held the cable operators responsible because they did not monitor their own channel systems and close each one off as the retransmission came to an end.

The copyright holders and theatre owners won. Cable systems were forced to monitor their signals and close down each channel as it stopped transmitting. The pirates were told they would face severe penalties if they broadcast copyright programmes and movies which were less than three years old. That was in November 1981.

Interest has subsequently died off. There are fewer pirates, though some have started making their own programmes. These are located close to Amsterdam. But many Dutch television critics say the whole process has softened up the audience for commercial television. Now there is a big push to put commercials on one of the Dutch stations. There is also talk of a Euro-satellite programme carrying adverts.

All this accompanies a general underlying crisis within the Dutch policy. Since the mid-1970s the infrastructure of Dutch society has been breaking down. It is still strong in rural areas and small cities, but elsewhere, particularly in the Randstadt, studies show people feeling more culturally at sea. Many have put this down to the effects of television. Others say it is political.

But, as one social historian in Utrecht put it: 'It is, of course, a relationship between these two and the economy which is getting very bad. There is less and less to go around. Holland has a growing unemployment problem. There is a feeling of terror in some areas. People are losing their community spirit as they become capable of standing by watching someone being attacked in the street.

This may not be new in other Western nations, but it is a new feeling of alienation for the Dutch. The first reaction has been one of conservatism. It will be a storm to be weathered. Commercial television seems to thrive in this consumer-individualised type of environment.'

Chapter 4
Japan: a yen for the micro market

Japan is a vulnerable nation. It has a huge population on a few islands with hardly any natural resources. Everyone is keenly aware that life amounts to one simple equation: you have to produce the goods the world wants to survive.

Having been divested of a world power role by the post-War settlement, successive Japanese governments have promoted national economic interests above all others. By contrast, Western governments continued a more passive role of setting broad guidelines for private industries – ground rules which tended to shift with the changing configuration of political parties. Only France has taken halting steps to co-ordinate state, finance and industry towards specific national ends, offering a direct alternative to the American challenge. And even then it was not until after 1981 that the state was given a firm upper hand in these operations. By that time the penetration of American technologies and corporate models gave little room for experimentation.

Japan, by contrast, accepted the inevitability of the American world market early, and set about making these forms its own.

The Japanese took US technological innovations and reproduced more of them cheaper than American corporations. They wedded American three-tier corporate organisation with an inherited industrial structure containing a few giant corporations integrated vertically and horizontally. By 1981, therefore, Japan had already passed through a period of accelerated economic growth led by the electronics sector.

The central factor in the organisation of the Japanese economy has been the Ministry of International Trade and Industry (MITI). At the end of 1981 an internal political metamorphosis and the effects of deepening world recession had shifted MITI away from its pivotal position. A 'second stage' industrial crisis was on the horizon. But between 1949 and 1980 MITI was at the centre of national survival management, directing the focus of all active forces in society on to those few areas where Japan Inc. might compete successfully for market dominance.

MITI is small by comparison to industry ministries in the Western world. It is an elite collection drawn from the top families and management hierarchies, the inheritors of the Samurai leadership tradition. The men at the ministry managed the economy through 'Kondanki'. This is a peculiarly Japanese aphorism for a series of informal meetings between government, business and the banks which designate the sectors Japan is best suited to compete for, and organise corporate strategies to attain success.

As Toshio Takai, executive vice-president of the Electronic Industries Association of Japan (EIAJ), put it to *Business Week* magazine at the end of 1981: 'There was no mistake about our move into consumer electronics. In the 1950s we saw it could become the leading edge of economic growth and we started working towards that. The European and American electronics industries were paying more attention to military and industrial electronics than to consumer electronics. So that was what we decided to concentrate on.'

MITI and other government departments set aside large sums of money to encourage Japan's large electronics corporations to develop the skills needed for semi-conductor production. Banks were the principle sources of investment capital. This meant companies did not have to answer to shareholders on a regular basis. The semi-conductor industry took about 10 to 15 years to pay off. By contrast, bank loans in Britain usually run over five years. But by 1975 Japan had captured almost 95 per cent of the world market for semi-conductors.

From the outset these industries were export-oriented. When it came to moving into a new market with radios, calculators or stereos, relatively cheap labour costs allowed them to cut prices until the market was secure. The programme also had an important adjunct: the home market was closed off to foreign competitors with high tariff walls. It all added up to a closed circle of growth. Foreign technology was purchased and produced for the protected home market. This provided the cash needed to bump up production levels. When volume production became cost-effective the unit was put into foreign markets at low prices. MITI controlled the import/export flow by having sole right to grant foreign trading licences. No company could realise its final-stage profit cycle without MITI approval.

Despite this, it has been a mechanical industrial revolution riding the back of cheap, well-organised labour. The 'company' automated production lines to mass produce American innovations. The company developed a loyal labour force by managing what social services there were. The state has had little to do with these services. The company is both the giver and taker away.

By 1975 American semi-conductor manufacturers threw in the towel. They were in a fast-moving share market where their ability to raise money for expansion depended on showing high profit margins, fast growth and regular dividends. But the market for consumer electronics semi-conductors is a two-edged sword. For while it is tailor-made to the American style of corporate organisation, production and marketing it is also slow to pay off: the lead time before a return on investment can be five to ten years, consumers are very fashion conscious, and a great deal must be invested in market research.

With their requirement to satisfy a pushy stock market rather than more laconic bankers, American electronics corporations moved towards grant-aided high technology production, like satellites. With the US government also guaranteeing a return, the market could be mollified, and specific consumer electronics products could wait their turn. Most companies cut their production at the bottom end of the price scale. This left the door open to expanding Japanese corporations.

But there was another reason why the Japanese got the jump on the Americans. During the 1960s and 1970s the US semi-conductor and chip makers were lowering their labour costs and reaping high short-term profits by replanting their factories in the Third World, particularly Asia. They developed huge off-shore industries in places like Hong Kong, Singapore, Malaysia and the Philippines. At the same time the Japanese were digging deep into their pockets to make their own assembly lines fully automatic. It was a long-term investment made possible by the state's financing role. But it meant that when the American companies were looking to assemble more sophisticated systems, or when local labour and political situations turned against them, they had no way of maintaining their profitability. In the end, they had to bite the bullet and come back to America and start building automated factories. By this time the Japanese investment was already starting to pay off.

Computopolis: selling the interactive society

In 1968 MITI started holding some very important Kondanki. Experts like Yoneji Masuda were telling them that the market for the year 2000 was going to be in 'interactive information systems'; and if they were going to have a part of it they must use their lead in micro-chips and other semi-conductors to get a grip on the world computer market.

Masuda was a man to listen to. As Japan's leading techno-futurist he had produced the nation's first 'White Paper' on computer-communications in 1965, called 'The Plan for an Information Society: Japan's National Goal toward the Year 2000'. Since then he had been campaigning for a series of experiments in interactive communications environments sponsored by the government (see background note 1). At the centre of Masuda's world was 'computopolis', the computerised city. He said Japan could achieve what was termed 'a fully interactive urban environment' by the end of the century. He set 1985 aside as the 'post-experimental launch year'.

To MITI this sounded like good business. If the world was going to be 'wired up', Japanese industry with its dominance in semi-conductors, might be well placed to cash in. What was required was a new plan to reorganise the consumer electronics industry towards computers. In the end, the government representatives came out of their meetings saying they planned to have 18 per cent of the computer market in the United States and 30 per cent of the world market by 1980. This would require a two-pronged attack. Inside Japan, experiments in interactive information communities would get the go-ahead. They would also be evaluated with an eye to creating a home market.

MITI got six firms which looked like having the necessary skills in computers to agree to co-ordinate their activities at different levels of production, and to complement each other as much as possible in foreign markets. To get the ball rolling MITI threw in 300 million dollars for research and development between 1972 and 1976. (See background note 2.)

The Japanese electronics firms knew they had some special abilities to bring to this new challenge. They had a committed labour force, research expertise in micro-chips for consumer electronics second to none, and a highly integrated, automated, industrial structure. But if the aim was to move towards taking a piece of the world market for mainframe computers, with its high profit margins, there were two obstacles to overcome. Firstly, Japanese semi-conductor dominance applied specifically to consumer electronics. Secondly, Japan lagged behind the United States in the generation of programmes and software for these large scale computers. It was one thing to mass produce a microprocessor with a 'dedicated' programme to, say, operate a hand calculator or even make a computer compatible with an IBM machine. It was entirely another to devise original programmes and software.

MITI examined the world computer market. After 1979 it found that the fastest growing sector, particularly in the United States, was the 'personal' or microcomputer. A demand for these machines was now coming from small businesses and individuals. American computer companies were rushing to serve this market by opening 'computer shops' and 'computer corners' in banks and department stores. In other words, the microcomputer was changing the image of the computer salesperson from that of an 'office systems consultant' with an engineering background to a shop assistant with a knowledgeable patter based on a few company sales courses, a close reading of home computing magazines and an ability to size up consumer aesthetics. This new market looked extremely familiar to MITI: it had the same profile as the stereo-TV-calculator sector now dominated by Japanese companies.

MITI therefore suggested that firms with this sort of expertise should devote their research and development programmes to microcomputers. When they had the product they could go into the United States and Europe at the price-conscious bottom end of the consumer market. When the consumer was ready they would then 'trade up' to a more sophisticated product. This gave the Japanese industry breathing space to allow it to solve the programming and software problem.

In the meantime, MITI earmarked 50 million dollars for a three-year programme, starting in 1981, to encourage the growth of independent 'software houses'. There is a good base to work on. The prime computer manufacturers – Hitachi, Fujitsu and NEC – have had software research incentive schemes since 1970. At the end of 1981 there were 1,000 independent companies producing Japanese programmes and software. The larger Japanese companies, led by Fujitsu and NEC, have also simply bought out US software companies. When they have not been able to get their requirements 'off the shelf' they have set up a subsidiary and hired US programme writers.

Another national priority decided by MITI was on satellite technologies. Satellite broadcasting was about to come of age in 1979 and at least one company, NEC, was boasting it could provide all the systems needed to manufacture, launch and receive communications from satellites. A space programme was therefore set in motion, with the aim of having Japanese rockets launching Japanese communications satellites by 1986. The hoped-for side effect would be a Japanese proficiency in low-cost satellite receiving dishes. (See background note 3.)

Futurology: the reaction at home

If Japanese electronics corporations do manage to crack the world computer-communications industry wide open they will have men like Masuda to thank. He may not have actually created the home market base, but his futurology has been essential to the instigation of 'social experiments' in interactive communications. The two main experiments are called 'Tama New Town CCTS' and 'High-Ovis'. Tama New Town, a two-stage experiment, has already received an 'evaluation', and the results are being used as the basis for High-Ovis.

Masuda himself has restricted himself to the direct results. Certain products will 'sell', others will not. The actual social implications are another matter. But one set of observers not convinced that interactive communications are particularly revolutionary are Tarja Crombers of

Denmark, a specialist in housing and a former United Nations consultant, and Swedish journalist Inga-Lisq Sangregorio. Their evaluation of Tama New Town, prepared for the Dag Hammarskjold Foundation of Sweden, makes interesting reading.

The Scandinavians quickly established that, despite the social goals stated in the research proposals, the organisers were quite prepared to admit that the experiments were mainly aimed at developing technologies and the possibilities for commercial exploitation.

They also found that the broadcast time available for the experiments was between 2 and 6 p.m., when the only inhabitants of the households in the guinea-pig town were women and children. They did a bit of research and found that although Japanese homes and families are small, women spend five-and-a-half hours a day doing 'housework'. They also found, in the official statistics, that television watching amongst Japanese women had gone up between 1960 and 1975 from one to that magic five-and-a-half hours a day. They talked to a few people and found that this had occurred not because television was interesting but because there was nothing else to do besides boring housework. Even the Japanese broadcasting company's own evaluation of the project said that 'neither the content nor the availability of information was valued very highly'.

One big success in the experiment was the television camera installed in some households. Housewives could televise themselves and see their friends. They could even make new friends. The women were excited with this because it broke down the isolation they felt at home with nothing to do. But although this result evidently came as a big surprise to the male researchers monitoring the project, none of them thought it of great importance. They carried on programming information and entertainment around 'local matters' (When was Tama New Town built? When do the shops close? How do you call the fire department?).

Crombers and Sangregorio started wondering why more Japanese men were not involved in this experiment at the receiving end. They were even more interested in this lack of men when they read in government statistics that between 1967 and 1978 the number of men who thought their work was the most important thing in their life had dropped from 58 to 37 per cent. There were therefore a lot of men becoming more leisure oriented.

They talked to Japanese social workers and looked at more statistics. It became clear that there continues to be one fundamental characteristic of Japanese life underwriting every level of experience: the segregation between the man's world and the woman's world. 'The Japanese woman is still securely tied to the home by many invisible bonds', they wrote. 'The strongest ones are the lack of opportunity for professional activity and the lack of child care facilities and other social services. Other problems are the long working days and the tiresome commuting in metropolitan areas. And last, but not least, there is the social pressure; and its effect on a Japanese woman's expectations of her role and behaviour. . . . In 'the experiments – not by design, but in practice – have had women as the target group. From the woman's point of view this application of technology doesn't imply any revolutionary structural form. Woman's place is still in the home, to which she is now tied not only by all the invisible bonds we described earlier but also by ultramodern optical fibres. She gets more of something she already has a surplus of: household appliances and TV services. The only positive factor is the chance to see the neighbours on TV, and in that way to get to know somebody else in the area where she spends 24 hours a day'.

Despite such fundamental social criticism, as far as Masuda is concerned it remains now to see only which kind of terminal will win out in the long run. The competition is between micro-computers and viewdata terminals. The first is currently more expensive than the second, but with the cheapening of miniaturisation both will come equal by the year 2000. Throughout his projections Masuda also bases his figures on two factors: continued economic growth and relative stability of social form.

But already, within Japan, there are signs that these two important factors are becoming unstable. The Japanese economy is not growing the way government economists had thought it would. Predictions for the year 1980 were for an overall 5 per cent increase, yet when the final figures came in, growth was running at a poor 3.8 per cent. Other sectors of the economy are suffering from the general downturn in the world economy, particularly petrochemicals and shipbuilding. The nation is carrying a 61 billion dollar budget deficit. In 1981 this led to a refusal to cut taxes or increase spending on social services – including, ironically, housing in new towns scheduled to receive interactive communications systems.

At least one economist, Akio Kohno at Daiwa Securities, is saying that Japan will suffer economic stagnation by 1985. He says that a combination of new Western trade barriers and a more expensive yen will make the nation's electronics products uncompetitively expensive overseas. At home, wages will rise, pushing wage-earners into higher tax brackets, thus limiting their ability to buy consumer goods. All this, he predicts, adds up to a period of zero growth and an exhumation of those social and economic contradictions which have been hidden during the boom years.

Cracks in the Far East Bubble

On June 22, 1982, Tomizoh Kimura, a representative of the Mitsubishi company, was stopped by customs officials just before he boarded a flight from San Francisco to Tokyo. He was hustled into a back room where FBI officials took from his baggage some magnetic tapes containing diagnostic software for an IBM computer system. He was charged with industrial espionage and remanded in custody. On the same day six officials from Hitachi, including senior engineer Kenji Hayashi, were arrested in a swoop through 'Silicon Valley' around San Francisco and Santa Clara.

The action capped a bizarre ten-month escapade during which the FBI set up a phoney software secret agency to trap Japanese computer companies ready to buy IBM inside information. It opened a new era in Japanese-American trade relations and proved just how desperate Japan is to keep pace with developments in computer technology.

'This sort of thing goes on all the time,' commented one Silicon Valley executive. 'We've heard rumours of East European industrial spying for a while. Everyone knows there is a certain amount of design pinching, but no one expected two of the biggest firms in the field to get caught flat-footed.'

For 14 years various computer companies have taken IBM through a series of court cases to attempt to make them publicise their designs as soon as new products are announced. They failed. 'It's a fact of life that IBM controls 60 per cent of the world market for memories and mainframes,' said the executive. 'It's not a competitive environment. If you want to sell anything you almost have to make your computers interchangeable with those of IBM. The Japanese have made this their priority in the top end of the market.

'At stake for Hitachi and Mitsubishi was a completely new line of IBM machines that are simpler in construction, yet more than twice as fast at doing the job. If the Japanese were going to produce a competitive machine, even two years down the road, they had to have information on their internals as soon as possible.' Hitachi, in fact, gave FBI agents posing as computer secrets salesmen more than half a million dollars. The agents insisted that high officials of the company be brought into the scheme. The company was eager enough to send over some top operators from Tokyo.

This burning need to steal a march on IBM is not, however, just another chapter in the long saga titled 'IBM versus the rest of the world computer industry'. During 1981 and 1982 established home supports for Japanese industry have gone through some shuddering changes. There is a new air of insecurity about, leading to some panicky management decisions. And while the Japanese economy is feeling the first real effects of world recession, MITI itself has had its teeth pulled. Many companies have been cut loose to fend for themselves.

Throughout its history the secret of MITI's effectiveness with its Kondanki has been the bottom-line coercive power of export licences, if a company did not have one of these licences it could not buy raw materials overseas or sell finished goods in foreign markets. In effect, MITI could decide who was going to do business where. But in December 1980 that power was withdrawn by a government now forced to cut back across the board on all its cash-associated incentives. There is still a flow of research and development money from MITI, but other departments are not being so open-handed with individual banks and specific industries.

In the short term Japan's leading electronics and communications corporations have not been deeply affected. Consumer electronics products have generated a cash surplus available for future endeavours. But looking to the long term the company accountants have started suggesting that finance departments search out other sources of capital. During their quest, investment sleuths have discovered the stock market, particularly convertible debentures, which can be sold to prospective shareholders at pay-back rates lower than current bank interest rates.

Shareholders are notoriously fussy. They want to see balance sheets. They like to get dividends on a regular basis. They demand growth, and if it doesn't seem to be happening fast enough they start asking managers embarrassing questions. It's a new kind of environment for most Japanese executives. There are signs they don't quite know how to deal with it yet.

As one London computer stock analyst put it: 'There is a hint of shrillness to the normally smooth, integrated Japanese approach to foreign markets these days. If there is really going to be a period of zero growth forcing the government to run up the shutters on the pay-out window, the way in which these companies compete will start to change. Already various agencies, including MITI, have had to caution some companies about playing out their aggressive tactics on each other. MITI set them up to move into computer-communications; now the same organisation seems to be cutting the normally safe ground from underneath them.

'All this might be a passing cloud on the horizon. Japan has heavy investments in fifth generation computers, and most of the electronics corporations are cash rich. They may be able to weather the current economic storm. But no matter what happens, life for the computer-communications companies will never be the same again. There will be no easy march into the future.'

Background notes

Background note 1
Stepping Towards the Year 2000

Extracts from 'The Information Society as Post-Industrial Society', Yoneji Masuda, Institute for the Information Society, Tokyo, 1980.

During the late 1960s and early 1970s Masuda engineered the introduction of a nine-point plan designed to demonstrate the capabilities and rewards of an information society. He introduced it in this way: 'If the goal of industrial society is represented by volume consumption of durable consumer goods or realisation of heavy mass consumption catering around motorisation, information society may be termed as a society with highly intellectual creativity where people may draw future designs on an invisible canvas and pursue and realise individual lives worth living.' Masuda's 'demonstration' projects were to come in two stages, the first between 1972 and 1977, the second carrying on towards 1985.

(1) *Administration 'bank'* (Cost: 3 million dollars): This would hold all government records, beginning with a listing stretching back ten years. It would also hold a 'policy' module and policy programmes which could be assessed by any level of public office.
(2) *Computopolis Plan* (1.1 billion dollars): Computopolis is a computerised city with cables delivering 'core' information services and interactive capabilities. Two schemes of this type were started (see Appendix XI).
(3) *Regional Remote Medical Systems* (277 million dollars): A 'completely automated' hospital interacting with a local population of about 100,000 and serving remote island communities. Office, diagnostic treatment and clinical studies will be peformed.
(4) *Computer-oriented education* (266 million dollars): From a university computer centre the education of children could be executed, measured, analysed and reprogrammed. Links would be facilitated by computer terminals reaching into every classroom.
(5) *Pollution Prevention System* (584 million dollars): A computerised monitoring, warning and control system for an industrial district.
(6) *Think-Tank Centre* (386 million dollars): All 'think-tanks', governmental and private, would centralise their data bases in a Tokyo office building offering 'research facilities'.
(7) *Small Enterprise Project* (127 million dollars): Introduction of 'management information systems' to a selection of 10,000 small and medium-sized businesses. They would receive terminals connected with a corporate management service centre.
(8) *Labour Redevelopment Centre* (179 million dollars): For retraining middle-aged and senior citizens.
(9) *Computer Peace Corporation* (10 million dollars): A team of systems analysts, programmers, engineers and managers from the electronics sector brought together to try to deal with problems of Third World underdevelopment and obstacles to world peace.

Background note 2
Organising Industry to create a Japanese World Computer Market

Japanese electronics manufacturers have two strong points, both brought about by a world lead in factory automation: consumer electronics (stereos, calculators, television sets) and semi-conductor production (the micro-chips and micro-processors which go into every electrical product). When the decision was made to lead the economy into the 21st century with electronics, certain strategies were arranged to build on those two strong points.

1. The four main computer manufacturers were 'aligned' so that they would not be competing with one another in research and development or foreign markets.
Fujitsu and Hitachi were aligned at the 'top end' of the industry: large mainframe computers. They were told to concentrate on IBM-compatible hardware (machinery which could be plugged in to take the place of functioning IBM machinery).
Mitsubishi and Oki Electric Industry were aligned. They were to produce smaller IBM-compatible computers. Nippon Electric Company and Toshiba were aligned to design their own computer architecture. They would move into mini- and micro-computers in the first instance, while attempting to puncture IBM dominance in foreign markets with their own mainframes.

2. In the short term it was seen that the best way to penetrate, or soften, foreign markets was to make arrangements with local manufacturers. This would involve a 'trade-off'. Local companies would get the benefits of Japanese 'cheap' end-products while the Japanese would gain a foothold in local markets for later expansion. Here are some typical link-ups in Europe:
● Fujitsu has local marketing agreements with companies in Australia and Spain. There are parts and machinery agreements with ICL(UK) and Siemens (West Germany).
● Hitachi has parts and machinery supply agreements with Olivetti (Italy) and BASF (West Germany).
● Toshiba has a five-year 'technical collaboration agreement' (signed in 1982) with SGS-ATES of Italy, for provision of microprocessors.
● Nippon Electric, using preferential development schemes, has opened micro-chip assembly plants in Ireland and Scotland.

3. However, the long term view of computer development is seen to depend on the mobilisation of Japan's lead in consumer electronics. MITI planners recognise Japanese effectiveness in the marketing of television sets and radio equipment through local agents, particularly department stores where products like calculators have been sold in a 'theatrical atmosphere' alongside personal and household goods. Strategists intend to wait until the personal computer has reached a stage where consumers demand a portable battery-operated machine close to the calculator. Then they will use their dominance in micro-chip manufacture (for example C-mos micro-processors) to package the product like stereos and cameras.

Already, in Japan, there are 63 micro-computer manufacturers competing for the local market. The leader is Nippon Electric with a 40 per cent share. This is closely followed by two calculator and micro-chip makers, Sharp and Casio. Both the latter have long experience in cut-price sales of electronic products, having used their low-cost production processes to capture 52 per cent of the world calculator market after 1974. The Japan Research Institute predicts that 50 per cent of micro-computer products made in Japan by 1985 will be for export.

Background note 3
Japanese Communications
Satellite Industry

Japan had a space budget of 481
million dollars for 1982. Its
programme is run through the
National Space Development Agency
(NASDA) and the Institute of Space
and Astronautical Science (ISAS).
Until 1978 Japanese satellites were
launched from the United States by
NASA. Now they have their own
rockets and launching facility.

Telecommunications Satellites:
1977
NASA (USA) launches CS-1 for voice
data communications, operated by the
Japanese PTT.
1983
CS2A will go up on a Japanese rocket
to replace CS-1. It will be followed by
CS-2B, a spare-in-orbit.
1988
CS-3 will be larger than those
launched before and will replace CS-2
with more capacity.

Broadcasting Satellites:
1978
BS-1 launched by NASA.
1981
BS-2 will replace the earlier satellite.
It is being built by Toshiba and
General Electric (US). This will be
followed by a second B series in 1985.

One Japanese company straddles the
computer-communications field in
satellite broadcasting: Nippon Electric
(NEC). NEC is the ninth largest
electronics firm in the world and
second only to Mitsushita in Japan.
But it is ahead of most, having
capabilities in both computers and
telecommunications.

NEC was set up in 1899 by AT&T. It
was taken over by ITT in the 1920s
and ITT still has a minority share. At
first the company specialised in
making telecommunications
equipment for the domestic market.
But later it became a world leader in
the manufacture of microwave radio
equipment for long distance
communications. During the 1950s it
invested heavily in transistor
production. By 1964 it was in the top
five world producers of
semi-conductors.

In 1982 NEC reported it was:
● World leader in sale of land-based
microwave equipment, holding 30 per
cent of that market not controlled by
national preference allocations.
● One of three or four companies in
the world capable of producing all
elements of satellite communications
systems, including the satellite.
● Holding a 40 per cent share of the
Japanese micro-computer market.
● Had an average one billion dollars
worth of consumer electronics sold per
year.
● Had overseas factories in Asia,
Latin America and the United States
making telecommunications
equipment, semi-conductors and
computers. Plans for 20 more overseas
facilities between 1982 and 1986.
NEC is also the leading Japanese
manufacturer of satellite receiving
systems.

4. Japan's computer competitors have
long derided this national thrust
because these automated industries
have shown they cannot generate the
all-important software which makes
computers at all levels worth having.
MITI has recognised this problem.
Three strategies have been employed.
(a) Computer manufacturers have
been encouraged to accept one
standard operating system for
inclusion in all machines. An interim
measure was adopted with the CP/M
system: this gives most
micro-computer users instant access to
thousands of off-the-shelf programmes
written for computers made by other
companies. In the long term MITI has
opted for the UNIX operating system
developed by AT&T's Western
Electric, which some say is the
forerunner of emulator
micro-computers, making the machine
itself less important than the software
available.
(b) MITI has provided large amounts
of money to help companies bridge the
software gap. In 1981, 150 million
dollars was earmarked for a three-year
scheme to experiment with various
operating systems. A further 30
million dollars was set aside to help
independent software design firms
come up with appropriate programmes
for Japanese machinery. There are
currently around 1,000 small software
'houses' in operation. Many are
subcontracting to the large, realigned

manufacturers. These manufacturers also have their own programmes. Hitachi has had a 'software factory' since 1969. It also owns 15 software subsidiaries. Fujitsu has 10 software 'plants', six established after 1979.

One Hitachi executive noted that most US software has been developed on the back of defence and space contracts, while Japanese applications are going direct to commercial requirements. Two thousand software packages are now available for Japanese micro-computer owners. The Japan Research Institute predicts the existence of 10,000-15,000 micro-programmes by 1986.

(c) Japanese computer makers still lag far behind with programmes for the larger computers, which offer the highest profit ratio. If they are to develop a world market by getting micro-buyers to 'trade up', they must provide distinctive software at this level. To provide the incentive the larger companies have gone on a hunting expedition for foreign software houses, particularly in the United States.

Nippon Electric is going the most direct route by setting up its own software factories in the United States, and hiring local wizards. The most successful of these projects is Information Systems in Lexington, Massachussetts, with annual revenues of 100 million dollars. All the other Japanese companies have gone the 'special arrangements' route. For example, Fujitsu has taken up two US partners, Amdahl and TRW, with software a major component in their agreements. Hitachi sells its computers in the United States through National Semi-conductor, which writes any software required. In Hong Kong it does the same through the British company Computerland.

Chapter 5
The Third World: spectators at the feast

Lesotho is a frustrating place to live. It is totally surrounded by South Africa. It has no substantial industry and its mountain landscape is ruined by overgrazing and fissured with ineffective colonial soil conservation projects. The capital city to the nation's one million inhabitants is a little smaller than New York's Kennedy Airport. One of its functions is to serve arriving and departing Western aid personnel.

The government of Lesotho comes from a clique of families who all went to the same five secondary schools. They squabble over foreign aid, direct projects to their own fiefdoms and form alliances around local rivalries between Catholics and Protestants. The army and police are small in number and can be brutal. Opposition was marginalised by a coup in 1970.

This is not an easy place to have a career in broadcasting. Radio – there is no television – is controlled by government dictat. No programming or administrative activity is so sacrosanct that it cannot be wiped aside in a moment by a Minister with a message for his people. Because of this, going to work is a lottery. One never knows what will happen.

It is also very depressing because nothing does ever happen. The radio station reproduces the current interests of Ministers. For the staff there is just no incentive to do anything but look as though work is being done and collect a pay cheque. Records can be repeated time after time by simply replacing the needle at the end of each tune. Technical operators will disappear in the middle of programmes, leaving participants stranded in front of 'live' microphones. Impromptu drinking parties erupt, reducing a day's broadcasting to fiddling a few dials on the control panel when passing through to the toilets. Broadcasters can easily become hardened drinkers: in one month during the spring of 1979 a journalist or broadcaster a week was killed in alcohol-related road accidents.

The two broadcasters on loan to the British Council were more than a little bemused. They'd seen it all before. No matter how much was given to these people they never seemed to make the grade. Back from a 'fact-finding' tour of transmitter and studio facilities throughout Lesotho they were relaxing on a soothing green lawn discussing their recommendations.

'We'll have to train a few in London, of course. But it's difficult to say what else could possibly turn around the appalling operational situation here. We can give them all the machinery they need but it's no use if they're too drunk or indifferent to get a grip on programming.'

These are not hypocrites or self-serving neo-colonialists out for some easy money and cheap holiday in a warm place. They're part of an army of well-meaning broadcasters, engineers, journalists and administrators who usually take a cut in pay to do consultancies or long-term contracts out of a feeling that in some small way their action might contribute to the improvement of our imbalanced world. They believe that a free flow of media into the Third World will help lift millions out of ignorance, poverty and their associated ills by throwing open a window on the opportunities this world has to offer to the 'less fortunate' of each nation.

Some come through the auspices of the major media and telecommunications institutions in the world: the BBC, the French ORTF, British Telecom, and from AT&T, NBC and CBS in the United States. Other consultants are seconded through national aid agencies or are part of the United Nations Scientific and Cultural Organisation (UNESCO) programmes.

They are also dismayed by what they find. Most broadcasting organisations are shot through with nepotism. The media serve the state first and foremost. In some places the state uses the media to enforce security aims. One way or another the consultants find it very difficult to orient their programmes towards that vast Third World audience. In the end, these experts are reduced to making short-term technical improvements, and they return to their Western jobs embittered by the unwillingness of the Third World to help itself.

After these experiences it is hard for Westerners to question the simple logic of a free flow of information and communications. In their societies they believe it to be associated with a levelling of authority, the development of professional probity and a commitment to education and entertainment designed for large audiences to take part in social and economic progress. If the free flow of information since the late 18th century has brought progress in the West, they figure it should work the same way for the Third World.

But to the bewilderment of these Westerners the Third World just seems to want to go in the opposite direction. Far from welcoming the free flow of information they call it a 'doctrine' manufactured as one of the tools of 'oppression' through which the 'neo-colonial' nations of the North, with the assistance of their 'multinationals', can keep the Third World in a backward or 'underdeveloped' condition. The incredulous Westerners are more inclined to believe that this rhetoric is being used by those self-serving government cliques to extend their hold on their people by barring outside ideas from getting into local media.

After all, they've watched with growing alarm throughout the 1970s as representatives of the Third World nations have used their numerical majority in various international forums to politicise what had previously been considered 'neutral' activities. Things came to a head during 1974 when an international agreement was pushed through the United Nations pledging agencies associated with it to work towards a New International Economic Order. The method would be a redistribution of wealth through regulation of trade and other relations between Northern and Southern nations. During the 1970s the idea was extended to UNESCO, where the body formally pledged itself to work for a New World Information Order in 1978.

The argument inside UNESCO went that the domination of all structures and resources of communication by the agencies (private and public) of the 'developed world' was detrimental. It distorted a nation's image of itself by marginalising 'news from the provinces'. Training for communicators (both 'technical' and 'creative' personnel) was conducted by Westerners, usually in Western countries. This training instilled 'professional', 'ethical' and 'economic' priorities often at variance with a nation's constitution, 'popular social predilections' and basic economic development priorities.

The Western media were said to set the 'cultural agenda'. Traditional values nurtured in village, family, community and nation were being eclipsed. In their place an 'international culture' held up urban, individualistic, un-neighbourly and cynical anti-nationalist images of life as those to which people must aspire to become modern. Finally, the ownership of communications technologies by Western powers was said to mean that any reform which did not put power over these technologies in the hands of the people of the Third World would only complicate the problem.

As a first step, the nations of the Third World sought to establish their 'freedom to decide' as a foundation for all future communications relations between themselves and the Western media. Next, they set about constructing a new aid agency, the International Programme for Development Communications, under the auspices of UNESCO. The agency would assist Third World governments to formulate 'culture and communications policies'. It would also provide money and expertise to follow through on these policies with independent media organisations.

'It's all polarised now,' said Canadian UNESCO consultant Tom McPhail in 1981. 'The old notion of a neutral international civil service is going down the drain. All the old guard Western staffers who rose to position through professional excellence and humanitarian zeal are being replaced by low level diplomats with a smattering of technical training and a big interest in seeing UNESCO push their own individual aims. It looks a lot like the extension of cultural censorship to an international level.'

Western news values, African politics

That's not the way it's seen in the Third World. Take, for example, a news reader in a West African country. He has risen to high position because his father is in the top ranks of the national security service. He got a private education, a degree in history and a lot of broadcast training in France and Canada.

'The only way to solve this development problem is to get all the Western agencies and their multinational corporations out of here,' he says. 'Once we've set our own priorities, got our land back to working without pesticides, built up indigenous financial structures, then we can deal them back in – on even terms. Right now we're in a one-down situation and no matter how good the product sounds it won't be made for us, it will be made for them and sold to us as an after-thought.' He was pretty drunk when he said all this. He is cynical and embittered. His broadcasting service was built by Western technicians. All the equipment came from France. All the teachers came from France. They all learned to make French programmes in French.

But this experience is no different from those 70 Third World nations who had their communications systems defined and developed in terms of the economic interests of France, Britain or the United States. (See background note 1.) The relationship continues. The technologies come from these 'old friends', so do the 'technical and creative experts'. Prospective broadcasters are trained by these experts or sent for a time to study amongst the 'old friends' and their allies. They return, pf course, with professional and technical capabilities and expectations incompatible with the reality of the national media structure.

Their Western journalistic experience has taught them to portray values in opposition to one another, to report the extraordinary, to edit for dramatic effect, to emphasise the role of the politician. Yet these attitudes, held without a balance of 'other ways of seeing', are anathema to governments desperately seeking consensus by highlighting the importance of 'doing something small but useful every day'. These governments want the media to emphasise the stolid yet 'heroic' consistency of a society 'in the making'. The role of the journalist is seen as a political 'guide' or 'teacher' who can throw new light on the 'united national survival programme' with well researched economic, scientific and technological material or simple exhortations giving new insights for the 'uneducated' by showing the problem and its solution in the exemplary life of 'an ordinary citizen'.

These things are expected of the West African news reader. But he does not know how to deliver them. He works in that sector of the national media system which has been left to replicate the model imported from France. He is closely watched. His Western training could be dangerous in a totally different political climate.

In this country, the one party state has a tenuous hold over a disparate population thrown together by illogical colonial boundaries. The balance of payments situation is wretched, so the state must force wages down in the small industrial sector in order to attract branch plants from Western multinational corporations. Food is always a touchy question. So much land has had to be put over to plantation crops to sell for foreign currency that the government has to import rice and grain into one of the breadbaskets of Africa.

Education is dicey as well. The whole structure of education, excellence, appointment and privilege is based upon a notion of moving from the periphery to the centre with diplomas from schools with courses written in Europe. This means the same faces that were at the top during the colonial era somehow keep popping up again and again.

Independence brought growing expectations amongst the population in all areas. Nothing very tangible has merged. There have been a few local uprisings and the government has had to invest money it doesn't have in military technologies. All this means that a good deal of decision-making about development is out of the hands of government and in the hands of the government's creditors – Western banks, multinational corporations and Western governments.

'We don't have the luxury,' says the news reader, 'of a multi-station, mixed technology, interactive information system. That's not only because we can't afford it and it's irrelevant to a population which spends most of its time eking out a living in the fields and factories, but because media, we are told, must be made to support the survival of the nation, and so must be developed in accordance with the needs of the state – which calls for a single-station, single-technology, one-way structure. Why the survival of the nation? Because we're at war – a war for the basics of life where all the weapons are in the hands of foreign agencies who sell them to us in return

for our cultural and economic sovereignty. All we have are human resources – people who must be mobilised and motivated to the cause of survival in the same way Western media rally round the flag and national unity no matter what the stripe of government during a war. If you tell me this is development I don't want it.'

Development has not been kind to this man. It has trained him to see the contradictions faced by his country in a way unacceptable to his government. He has been given a Western model for success and no possibility of achieving it in his own nation.

So he does his job. He edits wire service reports from Associated Press and Agence France Presse. He compiles press release on the movements of government officials. He listens to his version of 'truth' on the Voice of America so his news programmes will have a proper international perspective. Before he goes 'on air' he phones the Minister of Information to report the content of the programme for final approval. After the broadcast he gets drunk.[1]

But there are other, 'development', sectors of the media system in this West African nation. The personnel in these departments aim to guide, educate and 'animate' the people along the national path. These sectors are divided into 'projects', and since they are thought to be 'non-political', foreign aid money is lavished on them. The money is used to train local 'animators', and these people are surrounded with 'educational media technologies'. Equipment will range from printing presses to recording studios, slide projectors to micro-computers.

Sooner or later these media get people talking about doing things for themselves. Then the project is shifted to another 'high priority area' by the government. The work is not cancelled outright. If that were done the foreign aid money would be lost and the government would look less 'progressive' or 'democratic' in the eyes of aid-givers. Better to shift the resources. The important factor is that the 'vision of the future articulated by the state' never be challenged. Neither Western-trained journalists nor locally-trained 'animators' can be allowed an independent reign unless it adds force to the government's hand in a larger international poker game.

Third World United: the Intelsat deal

There is a rather sophisticated level of double-think abroad amongst most Third World government officials. They *know* what is happening. They know their economies are tied hand and foot to Western economic interests. They also know that if they are seen to accept this state of affairs passively they will be held wholly responsible when their nations dissolve into riot and starvation. They can see their natural resources being depleted, their economies going into hock to international finance and their cultural totems cast aside, while any semblance of social fabric collapses as too many people squabble over too few opportunities.

There are two things they can do. They can go for an individual deal that might help them survive until the next election, the next coup, or the next set of disasters. They can also unite with others in the same boat to maintain some 'respect'. If they have to deal with Western agencies and trans-national corporations at least they can forge a mechanism for saving face. If you can't be equal in fact, you may as well go for the fiction.

That's why there has been a mood of 'self-determination' inside the international organisations. So when the United States came to tell the Latin American countries how they would receive satellite communications, they had a framework for their protest.

When, in 1964, the Western industrial nations with Japan formed a club and set the rules for international satellite communications the Third World was excluded from membership. Nineteen nations, all from Western Europe except the United States, Australia, Canada and Japan, signed the agreement which created the International Telecommunications Satellite Consortium. As 'Intelsat' grew, membership *was* broadened to include Third World nations. The rules didn't change. The Third World had 10 per cent of global telecommunications traffic. It didn't count.

Intelsat was the initiative of the US satellite facility, Comsat. This is a consortium of government shares, publically held stock and shares allotted to the major US telecommunications corporations. It received half the equity in Intelsat. This would drop as others joined, but by 1982 the US organisation still had 30 per cent of Intelsat and was principal operating contractor, even though 105 nations were then involved.

The US Satellite Communications Act, which set up Comsat and empowered it to develop Intelsat, called for provision of services to less developed nations at a price they could afford. During April 1969 a group of Americans from the Ford Foundation, Comsat, Hughes Aircraft (who make communications satellites), General Electric and a few universities turned up in Santiago, Chile. They met representatives from nine major South American countries.

They told them they'd been talking amongst themselves back in the USA and they'd come up with a good idea. This was communications satellites. These were expensive to have channels on, but they were willing to give away some 'time' in a good cause. The American universities had come up with a plan to provide educational programmes on television to all the people of Latin America. These would be beamed via satellite.

There would be a special centre set up in Columbia, funded by the Ford Foundation amongst others. This agency would help make the programmes and combine the educational needs of the various Latin American nations. Each government would have the dubious privilege of awarding the contracts for ground equipment to the foreign corporations. Most of the money to pay the corporations would be loaned from Western nations or international agencies.

At first it looked like just another aid deal. Then the Latin Americans started thinking. These programmes, made in America, would be beamed to Latin Americans all over the continent. In other words, even though there would be time to help plan the programmes in Columbia, there would be no real control over distribution – local educational authorities would be faced with a *fait accompli*. It was one thing to allow indiscriminate advertising on local media – at least it was local production and consumption nominally under the control of the relevant media authorities – but quite another to be told that the educational and cultural requirements of a Columbian were as close to those of a Chilean as made no odds when it came to producing a series of homogenised programmes. The representatives started to have second thoughts. There would have to be more careful thinking about the requirements of each nation. As one Peruvian put it: 'We had just got rid of "Sesame Street" and were inching towards some sort of educational reform. We didn't want more "made in America" education, not just yet.'

But they had a nasty shock. The Americans suggested it didn't really matter whether or not each nation approved. Soon there would be direct broadcast satellites. Any school, mission station or village with the money to get a little dish aerial could pull in the programmes. This realisation had a unifying effect on the Latin Americans. No matter what the political configuration of the various governments, no ideological difference could hide the embarrassment of receiving a blunt ultimatum.[2]

It was pretty clear that if the Americans could do this with their satellites for education they could do it for anything else. First they set up an international communications satellite system with no Third World participation at all. Then they decide they can start broadcasting to the Third World anything they like whether or not it is approved for national consumption. It was a portent of loss of sovereignty so staggering that the Latin Americans were sent reeling towards the United Nations to try to save face.

By 1971, together with some 90 other nations, they had UNESCO pass a resolution that all satellite broadcasting into a nation must receive prior consent from the national authority involved. The only nation to vote against this resolution was the United States. For them it was the beginning of the long battle to save information from control by government authority. It hardly dawned on them that the deck had been so stacked against the Latin Americans from the start that they could not even point to some semblance of equality in the administration of satellite communications.

In the short term UNESCO did its own feasibility studies on behalf of the Latin American nations. An Andean satellite was proposed. But nothing came of it. No one nation had an industry capable of building even the ground receiving equipment for a communications satellite. All the corporations which did were contracted to Comsat. Even so, everyone realised they would have to get their hands on satellite capacity if they could, just to stay in step with the new tune being called in the North.

So, while the resolutions flew about UNESCO, any country that had the money or the means dealt with Intelsat. By 1982 145 nations were linked to the system, and 105 were members, many from the Third World. A further 40 lease channel space on Intelsat satellites and 16 pay the organisation to run their domestic long distance telecommunications system. Most nations have also been content to have contracts with Comsat-associated companies like Ford Aerospace and Hughes Aircraft. All the equipment is bought on credit, usually advanced by a Western bank. A few nations, like Indonesia and Brazil, are planning their own satellite programmes. Again, Comsat-associated companies will get the contracts.

The Indian experience: space satellites in a feudal economy

India, however, has tried to break the mould with its own satellite programme. As well as leasing channels from Intelsat the government has protected a domestic telecommunications equipment industry from outside competition and encouraged indigenous production of components for satellites and other communications components. (See background note 2.)

In 1981 the Indian Domestic Satellite System (Insat) went into operation. It uses satellites built by Ford Aerospace and launched by NASA. But a good deal of the peripheral equipment, particularly ground receiving machinery, as well as scientific and technological evaluations, are conducted by Indian companies and state agencies staffed by Indians. The network had, at the outset, 29 earth stations. It will service a telecommunications network which has been averaging a 10.5 per cent annual growth, measured in numbers of telephones connected, during the last 32 years.

The 1976-1983 Indian five-year plan set aside two billion dollars for telecommunications development. A large amount of this goes in contracts and incentives to the nation's major electronics manufacturers: Indian Telephone Industries, Bharat Electronics, Electronic Corporation of India, Hindustan Teleprinters and Hindustan Cables. The industry is prolific and profitable, and exports three per cent of production.

The government PTT, the Indian Post and Telecommunications Department, also makes communications equipment at four factories. It owns the Telecommunications Research Centre in New Delhi where Indian scientists have successfully adapted a 1,000-line electronic switching system to Indian telephone standards. But 'adaptation' is the key word. Despite a healthy telecommunications industry, and an over-abundance of scientists, India has not managed to innovate computer-communications technologies.

The telecommunications industry has in fact followed the trend set by the whole Indian industrial sector of buying technological innovations from multinational corporations and manufacturing them under licence in increasingly automated factories. The simple reason for this is that it's cheaper to buy new technologies at bargain basement prices offered by Western multinationals, who can write off research and development costs against state military contracts, than to sink money into local research and development. It is also more cost-efficient to put capital into automated factories than to gamble on having a relatively docile and efficient workforce in the future. The result has been a growing industrial sector with guaranteed profits in a protected national market where the number of jobs created remains almost stagnant.

Those people who do have jobs are a small number in proportion to the population as a whole. Their relatively high and stable incomes make them into an industrial 'elite'. This would not matter so much if the government was committed to the original concept of the five-year plan, where the state set the pace and the agenda for development, directing all other sectors that come in its wake.

But since 1970 the importance of the five-year plan has been reduced as the government began legislating to encourage the private sector. In the years since the death of Jawaharlal Nehru the private sector has had a greater say in the formation of industrial priorities, and those priorities have created barriers to entry into the industrial 'elite' for most Indians. Yet government incentives for industrial expansion have been provided in the hope that more people may become part of the industrial 'elite'. As more people have more money to spend, the logic goes, they will create a wider demand for 'things modern', beginning with electricity and telephones. This has not happened.

Even though, for example, there has been a 25-fold increase in the number of telephones over the last 32 years the population has grown by 87 per cent from 349 million to 658 million. The vast majority of people (77 per cent) live outside the cities, far away from the industrial sector. The government has also been encouraging factories into the countryside since 1970, mainly to avoid a small but well-organised trade union movement while maintaining a reputation for 'telling the private sector what to do'. But there is no expectation that the benefits of the industrial economy will reach the oft-quoted number of 500,000 villages before the middle of the next century – if ever. In 1980 those 500,000 villages lacked any electricity beyond an occasional loop of wire in the local landlord's compound. Most are far away from the telecommunications grid. If it does pass nearby there will not be a local switching exchange or any regional maintenance facilities.

In a bold attempt to bridge this unbalanced equation India, together with UNESCO and a group of foreign aid agencies led by the United States, launched a second satellite programme in 1973. Code-named 'Site' (Satellite Instructional Television Experiment), the project used channels on an existing NASA satellite to provide educational television programmes to selected villages throughout the country. This experiment had a lot going for it in terms of 'localisation'. Everything except the satellite was made in India. Village antennae were constructed from chicken wire. 'Barefoot' technicians were trained to look after televisions. But there were still mixed feelings about its effectiveness.

On one side of the 'evaluation' game board stand the development education experts. Most of these are based at Western universities, particularly in the United States. Uppermost in their minds is the technical efficiency of the project itself, and their reports, for the most part, bypass the wider political economy into which their educational experiments are placed. They are interested in the success rate measured in numbers of people made literate, falling birth rates, more hygienic homes and healthier children. To them any tool which allows access to a wide audience is helpful. Satellites offer the potential of the widest ever audience. They are all for it.

Their studies of Site are complex. They are prepared to venture an evaluation only after all the empirical statistical evidence is in. They believe there are definite possibilities in certain areas. There have been signs of a 'good take up rate' in some areas and less eager response elsewhere. There have been technical faults. But the bottom line is cautious enthusiasm. This is a tool the Westerners know how to use; it relates to the world they come from. They are comfortable with it and they are happy to be able to recommend its use in India. On the basis of these recommendations a section of the Indian scientific community is suggesting that the government reserve space in the Insat programme for a nationwide Site project.

A second group of researchers, funded mostly by UNESCO and a few independent aid agencies, takes a different position. They consider the social structures surrounding the introduction of technology. They worry about 'decentralisation', 'community democracy' and the need to blend traditional and modern values. They are more reticent about Site. Romesh Chander and Kiran Karnik, writing a UNESCO report on Site in 1976, felt the infrastructure of the rural economy, and the relationship with state services, were not equal to the task of integrating the things offered by Site. Their report also referred to the millions of dollars and large numbers of Indian development workers, otherwise engaged, who were redirected to Site. They could only remark that it was 'a gigantic case study to find answers to technical and programmatic problems in the planning, designing, organising and creating of a viable system of educational broadcasting by satellite'.[3]

In other words, the programme did not affect the feudal constancy of rural India. It was not designed so much for India as for the international community interested to have a general 'case study of educational broadcasting by satellite'. Meanwhile, the Indian government had taken the opportunity to shift financial and human resources from existing projects to this very 'visible', 'high priority' project. There is a familiar West African ring to this chain of events (see above). Other researchers from this group have been more strident, suggesting that communications satellites are a panacea for the Third World. As Alihu Katz and George Wedell write in their book 'Broadcasting in the Third World' (Macmillan, 1978): 'Satellite communications systems have become the status symbols of the 1970s in the same way that television was the status symbol of the 1960s . . . there is yet no reliable evidence on which the cost-effective application of these techniques can be based. Studies by the Indonesian authorities with the assistance of the Hughes Aircraft Company of the United States suggest that in a country with terrestrial communications problems on the scale of those in Indonesia "a satellite system could provide a national telecommunications service sooner and cheaper than any other system". But we know of at least one Indonesian government radio station that had to close down its transmitter because it could not even obtain a replacement valve.' (Page 242.)

The case for communications satellites in the Third World is by no means proven. They may indeed offer opportunities to bypass the 'cable hierarchy'. But, like everything else that comes from the North to the South, it is a foreign technology introduced into complex social, political and economic situations sometimes on the verge of collapse. The short term answer is that for nations with virtually no developed telecommunications infrastructure the use of a satellite is not cost effective when the actual conditions of rural people – the vast majority – are taken into consideration. More often than not an efficient radio service might be a more useful thing to develop.

Waiting for the 'phone lines

Yet there is evidence that the 'satellite option' is often taken up for rather different reasons than 'the greatest good'. As Katz and Wedell note in the conclusion to their investigation of Third World broadcasting: 'The indications are that the wish to exploit commercially and militarily the investment made in space technology is putting developing countries under pressure to buy more sophisticated and more expensive communications systems at a time when their existing systems are far from fully exploited.' (Page 241.)

That these 'outside pressures' direct the introduction of communications to the Third World is nothing new. What communications infrastructure exists in most countries dates from those colonial periods when the capital needed to be in touch with the Northern metropolis. Later additions reflected new outside economic interests. If a nation had commodities to sell, the corporations dealing in those commodities insisted on a link with head office. Somehow countries of strategic military or economic importance to the Northern nations have found grants and loans to maintain communication with a volatile hinterland or a watchful enemy.

But even then, outside lines go to the North, not to the country next door. Until 1975 it was still necessary to route voice/data communications between Lagos (Nigeria), a former British colony, and Dakar (Senegal), a former French colony, through London and Paris. It's still almost impossible to get a line between Cameroun and Kenya.

Despite its 30 communications satellite earth stations, 31 international switching centres, and 30,000 kilometres of transmission facility (microwave or coaxial), the Pan African Telecommunications Union still hasn't got a viable continental network.

Henri Lefebvre, a telecommunications technician in Gabon, says knowingly that 'something funny happens to the cables in the rainy season if they're not buried in just the right way. Nobody bothered to tell this to the locals at independence. Even today there really isn't the money to train local technicians. When a new set-up goes in it's usually on some sort of grant. The grant covers the installation, not the next year and the year after that when it rots in the ground. So when it breaks, everyone just waits around till the money is found to pay for someone to come out from Europe with the spare parts. That doesn't happen very often.'

In 1978 Cameroun's Minister of Posts and Telecommunications, E. E. Tabi, told a telecommunications meeting in Geneva that most of those lines were in urban areas anyway. 'It is constantly found that at least half the total number of telephones in the network of an African country are centered on the capital's telephone exchange, the rest being spread thinly over a dozen or so major towns and villages. The impact of the telephone on the countryside is virtually negligible.'[4]

Africa is worst off in the telcommunications stakes. But Asia and Latin America are not far behind. World Bank statistics show they have a higher telephone 'density'. But then they have more cities with more people in them. In fact the ratio of telecommunications to population in Latin America is roughly equal to that in Africa, despite the fact that Brazil is about to have its own communications satellite. And as anyone who has ever tried to get a line in Santiago or Caracas will know, inevitably 'the lines are always down'.

'They can wait hours for a dial tone and days for an inner-city call. Rush hour on the roads coincides with rush hour on the line, creating comparable chaos. The struggle merely to get a telephone involves bribery and privilege. There can be more people on the waiting list than in the telephone directory . . .'[5] 'It is therefore of first importance for African countries to have their own electronics industry.' That's what Mr. Tabi said in 1978, and it makes sense for the whole Third World.

An indigenous electronics industry should mean communications equipment purpose-built for disparate and challenging Third World environments, with lots of spare parts, trained local personnel, the ability to provide a communications system from taxes on the electronics industry and employment for a population demanding cash to buy basic needs as well as advertised corporate consumer products. Presto. It looks like

development. A healthy economy will create more industry. Soon everyone will be poised to buy themselves into the information age even if the
government is too corrupt or authoritarian to allow free flow of information in the first place.

This is just what the diplomats were thinking when they dreamed up
the New International Economic order and linked it to the progress of
the New World Information Order. If capital and technology flows are
monitored by international bodies to safeguard the interests of the Third
World and provide equal distribution of resources, and at the same time
other international bodies make sure communications developments are
organised to serve the needs of the citizens of the Third World (the vast
majority of whom live outside the cities), there should be no problem.
Back to the padded debating chambers. Just keep united and push for
'self-determination'. But no one really believes any of this, particularly
Third World politicians, diplomats and planners. It's one thing to campaign for a little self-respect, it's another to get what you need.

Diving off the export platforms

*The Mexican film-maker was smiling. A drop out from one of the nation's
top management schools, sent abroad by his embarrassed ranching family to
learn a trade, he sat now beside a bubbling tarmac road near the United
States border.*

*'When I was a boy my father used to crash through the underbrush of our
Yucatan estate patrolling for fire, with two Mayans sitting out front using
their machetes to beat a track. That was comparative advantage. We had a
jeep. We could husband our crop better. We had more of it in better
condition to sell. We could get a higher price.'*

*He paused and swept his eyes across the parched terrain to rest on a wire
fence and, beyond, a set of low modern buildings. 'That, too, is comparative advantage,' he said. 'That is an American electronics factory. We
attracted it with our comparative advantage – cheap labour and no taxes.
US companies put their assembly lines here. People wire together semi-
conductors. These things could go into televisions, they could go into computers. It's hard to know because the parts are shipped North for assembly all
over America. The only duty paid when the components leave the country is
on the value of the labour added in Mexico. A Mexican costs five dollars a
day. An American costs 75 dollars a day. It's our comparative advantage.*

*'Our economy, they say, has been growing fast since the price of oil went
up. Government agencies, local offices of foreign corporations, even our
own companies that sell things to the new rich people – they all want
efficient communications. Only the very best will do. Our new computer
experts do not want Mexico to appear "second-best" in the eyes of the
world. They know what to order because they have been working with the
most advanced machines during their training courses at the management
schools run by multinational corporations and universities in the United
States. Computers are in such demand, thousands have been smuggled
across this very border. Now the government has made new laws. The
number of imported computers must be restricted. So the foreign computer
companies have to start assembling their machines here.*

*'Of course the foreign companies are very cynical about this. They know
the Mexican industrial sector has not had any tradition of assembling these
machines. The components factories only make the most basic parts, some-*

*times simple frames bent out of sheet metal. But most of them have applied
for permission to operate factories here. They are openly saying they have
done this to play up to the current government, hoping that the next government will change the rules or make exceptions.*

*'But our government ministers are very positive. They say, now, that we
will have a computer-communications revolution which will crown our
expanding telecommunications system with its data networks, satellite
channels and direct lines to New York. It will take the place of oil and lead
our society into the 21st century.'*

*He rose slowly under the heat and headed South East. To the South
West the sticky tarmac disappeared towards the capital. Over to the East,
beside a rough track, a string of wood and adobe huts shimmered in a
mirage-strewn horizon. There was nothing else. Not even that American
perennial, the telephone pole.*

In the market of comparative advantage the Third World must live by its
geography or its wits, usually both. At one end of the spectrum stand
nations luckily placed on the globe to have oil or gold or some other
natural resource so precious to Northern industrialists that they'll queue
up at your front door.

At the other end languish a group of nations with barren land, nothing
interesting under the surface, and a population addled by near starvation.
Their representatives huddle near the edge of the marketplace like crip-
ples in the gutter banging empty tin plates.

In the middle are the dealers. Some have a small population which is
relatively well educated, or a large population which is relatively well fed.
Others have some natural resources and a growing population in the
countryside. Still more lie across traditional trade routes or in the midst
of East-West 'flashpoints'. There are a few with a small upper class,
grown rich on generations of plunder with the money to create a market
no matter what their geographic or demographic profile.

One way or another, the latest trend in industrial development is the
'export platform' or 'free export zone'. Governments promise to build
factories, offices, even clear out whole urban areas. Taxes are reduced or
waived altogether. In most cases the area of production is considered to
be 'offshore'. Anything made there can be taken in or out for virtually
nothing. Another guarantee is a submissive workforce without trade
unions, and a strong set of laws with force to back them up against any
nascent organised labour.

This nifty market loss-leader was developed in Mexico after 1960. But
the Asians soon made it into a full-blown economic system delivering
orderly, productive workers at extremely low rates. (See background
note 3.) The favoured commodity is young women from the countryside.
Electronics corporations have been big users of this commodity. They
like them between 18 and 25, particularly in Asia where they are considered docile and obedient with nimble fingers, sharp eyes, a high
threshold for boredom and without the strength to complain when their
wages stay low, or when they're laid off.

There are an estimated four million people working on export platforms around the world today. Most of them women. Most of them in
Asia. Most of them losing their eyesight in microelectronics factories.
The girls who thread the wires on to the silicon chips for interactive
communications equipment would probably never be able to see the

video display units even if they could afford them.

But what about development? Well, ignoring for the moment the repressive regimes, the dissolution of traditional cultures, a waterfall of humans towards already overcrowded urban areas, disruption of local food production, family separation and breakdown, and the emigration of badly needed professionals into the Western corporate structure, it looks pretty good for a few. The list of nations with thriving export platforms parallels the World Bank list of NICs (Newly Industrialised Nations) said to be in the fast lane of modern history. They boast growing telephone densities and local computer-communications industries.

The Brazilian experience: a micro-industry – and rising debts

Brazil, considered one of the major economic success stories of the post-War era, has been promoting an indigenous computer industry since 1974. In that year the state-owned 'Cobra Computadores e Sistemas Brasileiro' (CCSB) started making computers for the navy. In 1976 government officials at the Secretaria Especial de Informatica (SEI) decided the future belonged to the micro-computer. They determined that Brazil would have a stake in this future.

Foreign companies would not be allowed to sell micros in Brazil. They would be able to sell mainframes, where the profit margins are greater. If they agreed to manufacture mainframes in Brazil they would be protected, through import duties, from products of the same class made overseas. These companies, like IBM, Burroughs and Honeywell-Bull, would have to export as many as three out of every five of their Brazilian-made mainframes. The computer companies didn't mind. If their exports reached this ratio they would qualify for 'offshore' status and could claim many of the perks available in the 'export platforms', including a workforce tied to an average wage of one dollar fifty a day.

Meanwhile, in 1978, four local electronics companies were allowed to join CCSB in the protected micro-computer manufacturing industry. By 1982 there were 25 companies in the assembly business with another 12 or more making 'peripherals'. Between 1978 and 1981 16 per cent of the almost 9,000 computers installed in Brazil were made in local factories. This meant 8,000 jobs in manufacturing and 120,000 jobs in a growing information sector, and a small export programme. One company has a small research team and another has been selling micro-computers to China.

Brazil has financed this launch into computers by allocating Treasury funds to support job creation schemes, tax rebates and guaranteed bank loans. But Brazil is broke. It has the largest debt in the world. If it becomes effectively bankrupt it could crush the international banking system. It was poised to do just that towards the end of 1982.

The economic 'miracle' of Brazil has, however, meant very large profits for a very small indigenous middle class, four per cent of the 120 million population, and a massive transfer of wealth to multinational corporations and Western nations. The wealth accrues from those additional amounts of profit gained when a product is bought or produced so cheaply in Brazil that when it's sold in the Northern hemisphere it delivers a return very much higher than the same product would if it were made in the nation in which it is being marketed. The Brazilian government has been unable, more often unwilling, to extract this wealth from its own products when they are being exported. Instead it has generated the cash for development by issuing government bonds and loans, hoping that the small amounts taken in ordinary taxes and revenues from state corporations would cover dividends and loan repayments. It hasn't.

By the autumn of 1982 Brazil had a debt of 80 billion dollars. The state corporations, which dominate each internal industry, could not raise any more foreign loans to keep the industries going. This state corporate sector accounts for three-quarters of Brazil's debt. At the same time, no one is interested in Brazilian government bonds. So many have been issued that their real value is rated considerably below their face value. No one will accept dividends in the local currency. The Cruzeiro is over-valued against the American dollar and could become next to worthless at any moment. But the Brazilian state does not have the capacity to generate foreign currency to cover the bonds.

The state mechanisms are therefore stretched to the maximum. To change them significantly would mean massive currency devaluation, heavy taxes on corporations and exports, and a very much harder life for the Brazilian middle classes. There is no political will inside the military government for this option.

Instead, Brazil edges towards restricting the flow of money in society. This is called 'deflationary measures'. It means there will be less credit available. Capital-intensive industries, of which micro-computer manufacturing is foremost, need credit to cover themselves during the 'lead time' while their products are being developed, assembled and brought to the market. They also need to borrow money to tide them over 'cash flow crises' caused when state corporations, their major customers, cannot pay on time. Companies and individuals outside the state sector also need credit to allow them to purchase Brazilian micro-computers. This money is no longer available. There are, therefore, fewer customers for Brazilian micro-computers.

It's a vicious circle caused by a shortage of 'hard currency' in the system which can be directly traced to the state's inability to collect revenues in proportion to the 'real value' of the nation's major exports. Brazil has tried to create new industrial sectors, like micro-computers, while the right to revenues which might provide a solid base for these industries has been used as a bargaining counter in the international 'comparative advantage' game.

Back in the Brazilian micro-computer industry, a welter of companies brought to life with state incentives are fighting bitterly over the shrinking cash at their disposal to tide them over the current production/demand gap. In other words, they believe the industry should be restricted to a few companies. Confined to a 'monopoly' in this market the few companies would not face 'price-cutting wars' when they put their own prices up. Neither would they have so much competition at the bank. But the SEI is not prepared to do this. The government says it believes in a competitive environment. It says it is enough to be sheltered from foreign competition. Of course, as local prices rise Brazilian micro-computers become more expensive than those sold by multinational corporations. If these corporations were allowed into the protected market it would have the same effect as a fox in a chicken pen.

During 1982 it became clear that multinationals were beginning to crack the SEI ban. Hewelett Packard had been given a 'dispensation' to produce a micro-computer for scientific use. Brazilian micro makers insisted this machine was easily adaptable to business and research practices. IBM was permitted to import a machine from their new line of 'personal' micro-computers. It would compete directly with a popular local machine. There were no clear explanations for this shift. One journalist writing in the *Latin America Weekly Report* said: 'The manufacturers are happy to suggest off the record that the SEI is corrupt.'

Bernardo Kucinski, a *Guardian* (London) correspondent in Brazil put this sort of thing down to a broader bureaucratic malaise caused by impossible contradictions. 'Brazil's economy has reached strangulation point: a measure designed to help one sector damages other sectors, preventing the original aim from being achieved.'[6] Brazil's economic miracle is certainly winding down. Towards the end of 1982, on the verge of going into default, the government was toying with the idea of calling in the International Monetary Fund to set up a new consortium bank loan.

The IMF prescription for Brazil would be a 'dictated recession', according to economists working with the 'moderate' People's Party (PP). In 1982 the PP was one of only four opposition parties allowed to seek elected office up to the level of state governor for the first time since 1964. The opposition believes the first casualty in any enforced recession would be the 'youthful' capital goods sector, made up principally of the micro-computer industry. The second casualty would be the poorest working people of Brazil. IMF economists had made no secret of their displeasure with a law protecting wages paid to these people, many of whom are on the 'export platforms', from the worst ravages of inflation. They would join that one-quarter of the world population (30 million) living in what the United Nations terms 'absolute poverty'.

In practice, the opposition parties will have little effect on these developments. Even if they capture the governorships of the most populous states, the military government, embodied in the Democratic Social Party, still remains responsible for the national economy. It is more likely that trade union-or-organised protests will combine with opposition pressure to drive the military to drastic measures.

But even if these measures do not come to pass, a distinctive Brazilian micro-computer industry is now highly unlikely. It may squeeze through an IMF-inspired recession and stand up to encroaching multinational competition, only to be relegated to 'simply making the frames'.

Most computer futurists agree the potential of the micro lies in the possibilities for exchanging software. Once microprocessors are available to make software completely interchangeable amongst all brands of machines, the machines themselves will become uniform constructions, like unconnected telephones.

The software option

The importation of software into Brazil is already a brisk business. In 1981 the SEI was considering the creation of a software register, thereby limiting the spread of foreign software. But programmes of any sort are notoriously easy to smuggle on tape, disc or paper. The idea of registering software was also hotly contested by the Sociedade dos Usuarias de Computadores e Equipamentos Subsidiatios (SUCESU), the organisation representing computer users. And whilst SEI trumpets the need for truly Brazilian software, the SUCESU members are the customers. Non-government customers who aren't looking for credit are at a premium in Brazil. They have had a way of getting the government to bend in their direction.

Brazilian nationalists inside the government, for example, have been loathe to allow direct connection of individual computers through the 'phone system to international data networks giving access to foreign, mainly US, data bases. There were dire warnings about 'losing data to foreign powers' and 'becoming technologically dependent'. Nevertheless, by the middle of 1982 the government, under pressure from SUCESU and other computer-using groups, had decided to allow access to one of the US data networks, either Tymnet or Telenet. Even if there were effective restraints on software smuggling, an international electronic highway would be hard to watch as it delivered batches of interchangeable programmes to the micro-computers of Brazil.

Some say universal software will actually add to the revolutionary effect micro-computers could have on Third World societies. Industrialists in Japan as well as IBM researchers predict that interchangeable software will make the programming and operating of micros accessible to everyone at almost no cost. The programmes will show you how to write your own programme. Every local society could develop its own 'computer language', and the micro-chips in all the different machines would see to translation.

But this completely open-ended affair could work another way. The software will only be cheap in the first place if it is written for mass audiences – 'language zones' as some writers call them. The people with the best facility for producing to fit mass regional markets are the multinational corporations in the Western world, particularly in the United States. These corporations operate within an international economic environment. The structure of that environment, in so many minute ways, militates against an 'equal' exchange between Western industrial powers and the Third World.

Brazil is another version of that environment. In this nation, as elsewhere, something introduced to affect a straightforward social benefit is put through the prism of authority, corruption, inequality, brute force, industrial penury, urban squalor and peasant subjugation to arrive as a distortion of original intentions. There is just as much chance that the universal proliferation of software through the Third World will truncate local micro-computer industries set on a more traditional course of running the economic gauntlet from a 'hardware base' to creation of their own software.

As 'universal software' becomes the centre of the micro-computing system its worth will also rise in relation to the micro-computers themselves. Micro-computers are already considered to be at the 'bottom end' of the market. Profit margins are very tight. There is a need to sell a lot of machines to break even, or be allowed to share a monopoly in the local market.

Again, the nascent Brazilian micro-computer industry faces a difficult future. Government incentives created a gaggle of companies. The economy is going into recession. The market for the micros is uncertain. The government refuses to limit competition. At the same time, initial protection from multi-national corporations is faltering. All this is occurring while the worth of the product itself is falling. Inevitably, there will be a 'shaking out'.

The state and the banks will not have enough cash to save all the companies. Those with a close personal relationship with the dominant state firm will survive in diminished form; others will perish. There will be a legacy of Brazilian products with no existing parts and service back-up. Computer users will demand reliable machines for their universal programmes. As a result, there will be pressure to allow multi-nationals to move into 'designated' areas of the industry vacated by Brazilian bank-ruptcies. The Brazilian micro-computer companies will be left struggling to survive on low volume sales in a highly competitive profit-by-volume sector, dependent on state subsidies and recurring bank loans.

This is a scenario. It has happened throughout the Third World when governments have attempted to create local secondary industries to manufacture anything from bicycles to automobiles, tin cans to calcula-tors. It is a reminder that the overwhelming factor defining the future of the micro-computer industry in Brazil, as in other Third World countries attempting to build electronics industries, is the fundamental contradic-tion which exists in political and economic relations between nations. Third World countries are dependent for their economic development on the policies of multi-national corporations over whom they have little control other than the bargaining power they can mobilise around com-parative advantage. No amount of computing power, micro or otherwise, can change this underdevelopment equation.

Yet even in the vortex of these contradictions, the Brazilian micro-computer industry is an exception. Few other Third World nations can boast a high technology manufacturing sector producing finished goods of any kind, whether or not they are for export only. Most are clinging to their 'export platforms' like shipwrecked sailors gripping a liferaft. It's slowly sinking.

Treasuries are deeply in debt to foreign banks. There is no money for national communications systems unless tied to outside economic and strategic interests, thus endangering national communications and cul-ture policy. Workers attracted to the platforms are living in appalling squalor. They see all the corporate products but are paid so little they can't even get the necessities of life inside the inflation ridden zones. There is an air of restiveness. In the Philippines, guerillas are boldly operating in provincial towns for the first time in years. Elsewhere under-ground unions are spreading. Politicians are looking over their shoulders. They're spending more on military technology. Soon it will be time to call for unity at the international meetings, gain some self respect, make some excuses for home consumption and look for another market angle on comparative advantage.

The new communications imperialists: blueprints in briefcases

The Canadian broadcaster was home now, back from a planning meeting in Europe for the International Telecommunications Union. 'I really thought that was going to be a fiasco. They told us we'd been scheming to pack the committees with Westerners. They said we were moving un-ilaterally to allocate orbital positions and frequency specifications without proper consideration of their needs. Don't they realise these are technical questions?

'It's not our fault if most of the engineers are in the Northern nations. We've offered them training but this damn UNESCO stuff means we can only do it through their governments and most of those are so corrupt we never see the good ones, only the brother of the Minister. I don't know, ten years ago when we had these meetings we could get right into the nuts and bolts and have them worked out in a few weeks. . .

'They say they want time to do their own technical and social studies. I ask you, where are they going to get the engineers? I just hope this doesn't complicate the introduction of new communications satellites. We've got some real breakthroughs here. It's really exciting. It's something everyone is going to benefit from. Don't they realise that? What do they want anyway?'

In most cases what 'they' want is control – control over the pace, structure, content and effect of social and economic development. One of the tools of development is communications. To the extent that control can be achieved over communications, it is put into practice. To the extent that communications are 'tied' to the interests of other cultures and economies they will be resisted, even if it is resistance in name only.

This is why there is an air of confrontation over the allocation of radio frequencies, satellite orbital positions and the global flow of information. And these battles, carried out in the halls of UNESCO and the World Radio Administrative Conferences, have the potential to change the results Western nations and corporations expect from their own information revolution. It is also why there is an openness throughout the Third World to any overture which might carry the seeds of some actual transfer of communications hardware or software.

These communications components need not be linked into a network. They could include a micro-electronics factory, a computer assembly factory, a television 'network', a radio 'network' or a programme to send people for training in the West even if there is no practical use for their skill when they return. It might be a plan to deliver educational TV programmes by satellite, show movies from the back of a flatbed truck or give slide/tape presentations on basic accounting to nomadic herdsmen in their tents. It could be a series of agricultural extension radio programmes prepared by a multi-national team for broadcast to a nation with an average of ten radios per province. It could be an international programme to test the effectiveness of teaching literacy to children tending cattle on isolated hillsides by using books printed on paper that dissolves with the slightest hint of dewy damp.

It doesn't matter. What is important is the acquisition, in the name of the people, of each 'modern thing': the product of modernity for and by itself. The most up-to-date the better, so that it can be displayed to citizens and visitors alike as a totem representing the extent to which the nation has 'become modern'. This is the condition of the aid client.

The comparative advantage high rollers, who may be generalised as the Newly Industrial Countries and OPEC members, usually have enough clout to call for assistance tailored to their national aspirations, whether or not these take into consideration the actual circumstances of their citizens.

Another group, who have often fought a bitter war of independence and are described as socialist in the West, demand tailored assistance no matter how poor they are. They receive very little. For the rest, the vast majority of the Third World, international assistance is like a national health service which offers only one size of crutch. When these ill-fitting programmes are put into practice they do not always have the desired results. The priority for the government is the national plan and 'modernisation'. For the average citizen the aim is survival, betterment, as little disruption as possible, and maybe something nice to 'show off'. For the aid industry the aim is to have a successful project. These things are not necessarily compatible. The various parties may work 'hand in hand', but their ideas about why they are there, what they are doing and what will be achieved are often radically different. In each case the project will have profound effects upon the object of the aid, particularly if it is a rural community. Life will never be the same again. But it might not ever be the same as life in the next community or region either.

For the rural community communications aid has come in stylish waves, never applied to the whole nation, never maintained intact. During the middle of the century and up to 1965 radio was the system offered by Western governments and national aid agencies. Engineers, broadcasters, transmitters and programmes were all included in the package.

Television then became popular amongst the corporate research centres, educational foundations and aid agencies. Governments were offered much the same package as before, but built around television. They were told they should now be able to run the radio services themselves, that it was time to 'complete the transfer of technology'. Many of the radio systems fell into disrepair or simply atrophied.

Television offered new opportunities for education, particularly in rural areas, said the aid agencies. Here was a tool which could mobilise the hidden talents of villagers, offer stimulation to bring out their natural problem-solving abilities, give instruction on how to organise new self-help schemes, and provide a 'visual link' between educational resources and the 'village learning group'. Cadres of Western 'animators' roamed Latin America, Asia and Africa teaching village animators how to use battery-run television sets. Those countries that would not have or could not afford television were offered the same package built around radios, even though it was often portrayed as a 'second-rate' medium. But come the 1970s people were still living on the margin. Every available economic indicator showed that most Third World countries were worse off in 1970 than in 1960. This was despite an unprecedented number of development projects, particularly in the field of educational media.

There were a lot of opinions about why 'the projects were not a long-term success'. However, a general undercurrent began to spread amongst the development planners as the decade wore on. The epithet 'amateurish' started to surface at more and more international agency meetings. There was a feeling that the people who had been planning and operating the development projects during the 1960s had had stars in their eyes. These people, often dubbed 'flower children', were said to come from 'liberal arts' backgrounds and have no 'practical' knowledge of how to 'solve technical problems on the ground'.

Under this influence the aid agencies started to change their focus. Job advertisements now stated 'science' as a degree background. Engineers were in hot demand. Other agencies were looking for 'problem solvers' rather than 'teachers'. In the communications field the buzz word became 'infrastructure', as in 'What we need here is a grid system and a good signal propagation study'. It paid to have boned-up on a basic technical dictionary if you wanted to work in Third World development media after 1975. The corporate research centres started holding seminars with titles like 'Putting the 'phone in every village – the role of the village council' and 'Two-way satellite radio – the medical implications of service to remote regions'. It was clear that the plans would be visualised on blueprints in briefcases rather than posters in rucksacks.

Science writer and futurist Arthur C. Clarke signalled the emergence of this 'new phase' when, acting as a delegate for Sri Lanka, he rose at a UNESCO communications development meeting to say that 'the appropriate technology for the developing world is electronic digital technology. It brings forms of communication that are cheap and ideally suited for people who cannot read'. Edward Ayensu, director of the office of biological conservation at the Smithsonian Institute in Washington was more specific when he spoke to *International Management* magazine for their September 1982 edition: 'The Third World village represents a sophisticated memory bank awaiting an adequate information retrieval system and the technology to use it'. Ayensu has found the tool with which to unleash this potential. It's the micro-computer. He says it 'fits the current settings of developing countries better than people realise'.

A for Apple, I for Inequality

But other people do realise. Thomas Lawrence is one. He is European vice-president and general manager for the US-based Apple Computer company. 'The main role of the micro in the Third World,' he says, 'is in education.' Others see it assisting the Third World in the comparative advantage game. Julian Bogod of the United Kingdom Council for Computing Development (UKCCD) has advised Singapore to take up computers. 'Information technology,' he explains, 'is vital to a trading company such as Singapore, because effective trading depends on information technology.'

If the corporations, research institutions and development agencies are gearing up to deliver the computer, Third World nations would like to be ready to receive them, and they are using the United Nations to share their plans for integrating computers into national development programmes. The United Nations in turn is finding the Milan-based Intergovernmental Bureau of Informatics (IBI) to co-ordinate these planning meetings. IBI is staffed by men like Carlos Giuliano, who says that, 'if the Third World missed the information revolution, too, the gap between them and the developed countries will widen'.

There is, of course, no question of the Third World missing the information revolution. The question is the extent to which inclusion, beginning with 'development education', will continue the current unequal relationship between the Northern and Southern hemispheres. A great deal of economic evidence points to social dislocation and chronic under-development. Some Third World nations, clearly fearing the worst, are looking to the IBI to provide an arena where doubts can be aired and ground rules agreed, placing heavy emphasis on national development programmes. Another group is prepared to listen to the Western-trained scientists and technologists. In the face of the odds this technology just might be revolutionary, they argue. It just might lift the Third World into the future beyond all the contradictions. As Ayensu, who is also secretary-general of the International Association of Biologists and adviser to the Paris-based World Centre for Micro-computers, predicts: 'It is now possible to plan an economic quantum leap from village-based rural societies to the computer-based information society of the 21st century'.

Whether or not they share such complete faith, a fair number of nations are prepared to use IBI as a place to show that they are interested in this newest sort of development project. Sri Lanka, for one, sees the opportunity to dovetail the micro excitement into a bit of comparative advantage muscle-building by cultivating a 'natural aptitude for programming among its citizens and low wage rates of less than 100 dollars for programmers'.

Everyone will have a chance to put their case for micro-development at a United Nations-sponsored IBI conference in Havana sometime during 1983. One hundred nations will attend, 65 more than IBI's membership. That's because a lot of money is up for grabs. The conference will divide the spoils of a one billion dollar five-year programme to extend computerisation throughout the Third World. Most agencies will take a lead from the IBI conference, but some groups are already in the field. Foremost is the aforementioned Paris-based World Centre for Micro-computers.

The agency is the brainchild of J. J. Servan-Schrieber. It has come as part of the socialist package to put France in the forefront of world computing nations, with their own version of telematique competing for the conceptual foundation of the information age leading to hardware and software exports. The centre's first approach to the Third World will be to refine the micro-computer to the 'abilities' of Third World citizens. Of prime interest is the discovery of a computer language simple enough that an illiterate can use it to gain access to the data needed to move away from economic marginality. Experiments are scheduled for Kuwait, Ghana and the Philippines.

The first experiment, in Senegal, got underway during 1981. Jacques Diouf, Senegal's Minister of science and technical research, told *International Management* magazine that the project 'with 20 schoolchildren aged 8 and 9, in three schools using micro-computers, looked at how well they would take to programming and whether social background or type of school made any difference to their ability to use the computer. The children were able to master advanced mathematical theory with the aid of the computers'.

Already computer developers are coming up against some familiar 'human resources gaps'. Bogod at UKCCD laments: 'There are rarely enough skilled systems analysts, project managers or data processing managers. Once the experts leave, it's all downhill. Most developing country computers operate on limping systems because they can't get competent managers to solve problems that arise.' Adds Thomas Hughes, deputy director of another computer development agency, Data for Development, in Marseilles: 'If they encounter a problem they cannot solve, they may drop it.'

The New Age developers have discovered even more pesky obstacles. There is a 'lack of infrastructure', 'sketchy, unreliable telecommunications systems' and power cuts or power surges on primitive electricity grids.

The computers themselves and their programmes do not yet 'fit' the

Third World. The machines overheat. They need more servicing than poor nations can afford. They can't run on batteries. The software is 'complicated'. Researchers worry that they will have to start innovating 'local' computer languages while the economics of producing a mass interchangeable software cheap and efficient enough for schoolchildren and village illiterates to use must be produced across 'language zones', from Latin America to Islamic areas. And then, notes the puzzled computer expert, there are 'political' problems. Some nations actually maintain a 'continuing debate over whether the computer should be encouraged at all'. Other nations seem to be ignoring the micro-computer and the information age altogether.

At least one company, Apple, has already seeen the potential. Education is a money funnel in the Third World. It is one of the biggest growth industries in the international aid business. The simple reason is that education projects can appear 'a-political'. In other words, if you want to set up a village-level campaign to teach people how to run their own local economies and change their societies, you don't ask to do just that and receive money. You must present it as an educational campaign for village literacy development. Then local governments are mollified and the international agencies feel they are putting money into something non-threatening and non-controversial. Of course, it applies to other things. Textbook dumping and religious indoctrination are popular examples. It all comes under education.

Apple, eyeing this billion dollar market, wants to break into regions long dominated by IBM, Honeywell and other large computer companies. In Africa, IBM, CII-Honeywell-Bull and Burroughs control 80 to 90 per cent of the computer market. Until 1981 this represented a tiny mainframe turnover. But now there are people like Senegal's Jacques Diouf preparing to introduce micros into national school systems. There are computer salesmen floating around Africa with dollar signs in their eyes. Companies from the 'former mother countries' stand to gain the lion's share of contracts in the same manner as broadcasting systems were 'transferred'. Firms like Apple, therefore, have to run in front of the pack in order to guarantee themselves a piece of the coming action.

Apple's Lawrence says that any and all problems with the micros will be solved by the technology itself. 'The trend in both large and small computers is built-in diagnostics. They will be more robust. They will run on batteries, have touch-keys to minimise moving parts and will combine some two million bytes of capacity on about ten integrated circuits. Writing programmes will need fewer skilled specialists because the machine will automatically show what needs to be done.' When Lawrence talks about the next generation of micros he is talking about how his own company will be tailoring a machine model to the needs of the Third World aid-financed educational market.

The micro-computer has arrived in the Third World. It has great potential. Yet there are many prisms through which it must pass before its true effectiveness is known. What can be said is that its current manner of introduction follows the same pattern as previous and continuing 'development initiatives'. If it is not going to emerge as simply one more 'style' of technical 'dumping' by the Northern hemisphere on the Southern hemisphere there will have to be a clear analysis of the real structure of under-development in the Third World. There is no sign that the people introducing the micro-computer have a grasp of this underlining set of contradictions.

In the past, communications development in Third World societies has fuelled an implosion of disruptive social, economic and political effects upon the people themselves. Today, as Third World nations swell the halls of international diplomacy with their face-saving demands and voting power reactions, they are set to cause an explosion in the face of Western attempts to create and transfer the information age in their own image.

Footnotes
1. Five news agencies dominate the flow of information into the Third World: Associated Press (USA), United Press International (USA), Reuters (UK) and Agence France Press (France).
For example, In Africa Reuters and Agence France Press control the news markets in more than half the nations on the continent. In many places they are the designated agents running the national news agencies' international desk on behalf of the government.
They set the agenda for editors and journalists, who must report on the world and the region in which their nation is situated. The agenda reflects Western political, economic and 'news' values.

The documentation of this dependency is rich and varied. Some useful starting points are:
Oliver Boyd-Barret, *The International News Agencies*, Constable, London 1980.
Jeremy Tunstall, *The Media are American*, Constable, London 1977.
UNESCO, International Commission for the Study of Communications Problems, Working Papers Nos. 13–15, Paris 1980.
Tapio Varis, *International Inventory of Television Programme Structure and the Flow of TV programmes Between Nations*, University of Tampere, Finland 1977.
Elihu Katz and George Wedell, *Broadcasting in the Third World: Promise and Performance*, Macmillan, London 1978.
2. Armand Mattelart, *Multinational Corporations and the Control of Culture*, Harvester Press, Brighton 1979. Pages 84-5. Herbert Schiller, *Mass Communications and American Empire*, Augustus M. Kelley, New York 1970. Pages 140-5.
3. See the information on India in Joseph N. Pelton, *Global Talk: The marriage of the computer, world communications and man*, Harvester Press, Brighton 1981. I am also indebted here to Dr. Jamie Mackie who, at the time of our discussions, was completing a thesis on the economics of regional planning in South India at the London University School of Oriental and African Studies.
4. See the Telecommunications Survey in *New African* magazine, December 1979.
5. Telecommunications Survey, *The Economist*, August 22, 1981. Page 22.
6. Information for this case study of Brazil has been drawn principally from Latin American Newsletters. The reports referred to here appeared in 'Entering the Micro-computer Age', *Latin America Weekly Report*, Nov. 20, 1981.
Bernardo Kucinski, 'Bluff Will Not Save Brazil', *The Guardian*, London Sept. 21, 1982.

Background notes

Background note 1
Third World Broadcasting

'Importation of complex technology brings with it many associated constraints and needs: engineering and production staffs must often be trained in the country from which the equipment is imported; methods and systems of working are necessarily imported; and then there is the continued dependence of the importing country on the exporting country for spare parts, continued training, and the new generations of compatible equipment. . .

'It is important to note a further, less tangible aspect. This is the aspect of a particular model of broadcasting that may be termed the implicit set of assumptions upon which the model is based. This set of assumptions will include norms, unwritten rules, styles of production, values, professional codes and expectations, beliefs, and attitudes. These factors may be less tangible than others, but they are no less important. They are transferred directly through training, socialisation and expectation and indirectly as functions of the importation of structures, technologies, and content of broadcasting that originate in the advanced industrial nations.' (Elihu Katz and George Wedell, *Broadcasting in the Third World, Promise and Performance*, Macmillan, London 1978. Pages 67-8)

Third World Broadcasting Systems linked to France, Britain and the United States:

France
Algeria, Cameroon, Central African Republic, Chad, People's Republic of the Congo, Dahomey, Gabon, Guinea, Ivory Coast, Malagasy Republic, Mali, Mauritania, Morocco, Niger, Senegal, Togo, Tunisia, Upper Volta, Cambodia, Laos, Lebanon, Vietnam.

Britain
Botswana, Gambia, Ghana, Kenya, Lesotho, Malawi, Mauritius, Nigeria, Sierra Leone, Somalia, Sudan, Swaziland, Tanzania, Uganda, Zambia, Burma, Cyprus, India, Malaysia, Pakistan, Singapore, Sri Lanka, Guyana, Barbados, Jamaica, Trinidad and Tobago.

United States
Philippines, Argentina, Bolivia, Brazil, Chile, Colombia, Ecuador, Paraguay, Peru, Uruguay, Venezuela, Costa Rica, Dominican Republic, El Salvador, Guatemala, Haiti, Honduras, Mexico, Nicaragua, Panama.

Background note 2
Status of Third World Regional and Domestic Satellite Systems

Name of System	Areas Served	Status
1. AFROSAT	All countries of the Organisation of African Unity (OAU).	Possible operational date late 1980s.

2. ARABSAT (Arab Countries)	22 member countries of Arab League. At least one earth station per country.	To be operational in 1984.
3. BRAZILSAT (Brazil)	Brazilian Interior. At least 20 locations in Brazilian interior to be served.	Award of contract not yet made. Domestic service to 19 locations to be provided on 6 Intelsat transponder leases through 1986.
4. SATCOL (Colombia)	Colombian major cities and interior; plus offshore islands.	Award of contract not yet made. Domestic service to internal network to be provided on 4 Intelsat transponder leases through 1986.
5. INSAT (India)	India and Indian offshore islands.	First satellite to be launched in 1982. System to provide telephone, data and community television to network of several thousand earth terminals. Second launch planned for 1983/84.
6. ISCOM (also known as Apple India)	Experimental project for India. (Ariane Passenger Pay Load Experiment.)	Launched in 1981. Solar array deployment problem, limited effective capacity of this satellite.
7. PALAPA A & B (Indonesia)	Indonesia – plus some service to ASEAN countries of Malaysia, Philippines, Singapore and Thailand.	2 Palapa A satellites launched in 1976/77. Network of 40 earth stations. 2 Palapa B satellites to be launched in 1982. Large number of 4–5 meter earth stations (18–22 db/k) to be deployed for Palapa B.
8. SATMEX (Mexico)	Mexico – telephone, data and TV distribution to remote areas.	This satellite would be launched in mid to late 1980s. RFP not issued. Domestic service to a network of more than 100 earth stations will be provided through the lease of 6 Intelsat transponders through 1986.
9. PRC (People's Republic of China)	China's major cities and remote areas.	This system has been indefinitely postponed. A lease of 1 to 2 Intelsat transponders will provide interim service until a decision is reached to proceed with the PRC system.
10. STW 1, 2 (People's Republic of China)	China's major cities and interior.	Launch dates are uncertain at this time.

124

Background note 3
Let's make a deal

Most Third World nations offer some
incentive for northern industrial
corporations. A few years ago the Max
Planck Institute of Germany found
103 nations competing in the
marketplace, all with varying degrees
of success. Some, like Chad, get one
factory (in this case a shoe factory).
Others, like Singapore, now have
more than 50 per cent of their
economies put over to export
platforms.

There are eight basic incentives. They
are manipulated by each nation into
various packages:
Exemption from duties and taxes on
machinery and raw materials.
A Five- to ten-year income tax waiver.
Exemption on all foreign exchange
controls.
Special project financing.
Provision of industrial estates
complete with factories, offices, and
support services.
Special controls on labour – right to
strike usually revoked.
Guaranteed low wages.

The Development of the Export
Platform has occurred as a sort of
panacea for quick-fix 'modernisation'
– each nation has sought to attract
companies at any price so that the
marginally increased spending power
created by wages together with money
pumped in by the companies
themselves might allow the purchase
by the state and new consumers of the
trappings of the modern world – from
shoes to bicycles to radios to
televisions to telecommunications
systems.

Chapter 6:
The UK: cabling up for the depression

The Edinburgh International Television Festival had been running alongside the venerable Scottish cultural jamboree for seven years when, in 1982, they came up with a snappy news title on 'Television in Transition'. For the organisers this was more than just playing with words. Over the years this gathering of broadcasters and their political friends had always been discussing changes they already knew a good deal about. This time they knew nothing about what was going to happen to British television – and it showed.

One broadcaster, overheard on the steps leading to the BBC studios, said: 'I've heard enough here about cables to do me a lifetime. It's so boring. It's got nothing to do with programmes. I'm going for a drink.' Boring it was. This was because the people talking about the 'new age' of television all had a piece of the puzzle, but no one had the whole picture. Whenever that picture emerged no one could see it, or they were unwilling to acknowledge it was there.

The organisers had invited a smattering of Americans. The transition seemed to be happening there. Maybe they could give some clues. But the people that came along just didn't seem to be 'the right sort'. There was Ted Turner, a cowboy from Atlanta who was pirating programmes and selling advertising for a satellite relay all over America and making himself a millionaire. He was smart but unscrupulous. There was a man in a silver jumpsuit from Manhattan who called himself ugly George and said he had the most popular independent cable programme in America. He made pornographic films of women he accosted on the streets. He insisted on interrupting the debates with the bland assurance that 'it's all about greed'.

There was a slightly 'more like us' woman from an American cable television network who bored everyone with a hopelessly garbled financial analysis of commercial programming. There was Fred Friendly, a jocular former head of CBS news and a professor of journalism, telling horror stories about the mess which might be made of cable television. He said the assembled broadcasters had to start educating each other about this 'revolution' – he seemed to miss the point. No one was quite sure what the revolution was all about.

All the same, these people, each in their own way, embodied the new media era. When they mentioned 'home banking' in the same breath as telefilms they might have seemed to be mixing metaphors. But they were actually visualising the all-encompassing nature of the 'home information/entertainment centre'.

Ugly George, with his video camera lashed to the frame of a rucksack just in case he might come across a willing female, was slimy but forthright.

'The only reason Americans went for cable was so they could choose not to watch Network schlock. As soon as they got that freedom they chose Tits 'n Ass. The big corporations saw there was money to make in cable so they started cleaning up its image with sports and schlock entertainment.

'In the beginning the free cable programmes were sleep music. You know, anyone could apply for time on the local channel. It was in the contract with the city. There was absolute freedom. Anything went. There were lots of talking heads, lots of family pictures, a few attempts at art movies. About that time I was taking photographs for the porno magazines. I got a video camera and went out into the streets. Now some people say I get women to undress right in the street. That's not true. I'll talk to them for a while, then we go somewhere private like behind an elevator shaft in an office building. At first I had a take-up rate of one in ten. They were all kinds – teachers, schoolgirls, women with children, everyone was curious. These days I guess the novelty has worn off. I only get a yes about one in a hundred.

'But I've got the most popular independent programme on cable television in America. You see you've got to realise cable TV is about one thing, profit. It's the free market. People can choose what they want to watch and they'll pay for it. If you give them what they want you make a lot of money. Whenever they've had the freedom to choose, people have chosen sex. It's as simple as that.

'The biggest joke about this place (Britain) is that it's completely unfree. Anywhere where the guy running the chief regulatory agency (the IBA) can get up and say 'We'll wait out the winter on this one' is not the sort of place where there is going to be action following words. There's just words. It's a talking shop going nowhere. Nothing really serious will happen because the government holds all the cards. Bringing in new communications here doesn't mean more freedom, it means more ways for the government, its supporters and its paid employees to foist their own ideas on everyone else.'

Whether or not Ugly George had a point no one in Edinburgh was about to take his word for it. It was clear enough to anyone listening to the Americans struggling with definitions and superlatives that this was a powerful and unknown quantity. For that reason alone it should be controlled and allowed to develop very slowly indeed. The question was who would control it and what would those controllers allow.

Lord Thomson from the IBA thought his organisation was best qualified. 'The IBA desires to protect national standards of British broadcasting and integrate new things with these valuable traditions. Whether or not Parliament sets up a new quango to regulate and introduce cable television the only group of people with the professional experience in that sort of regulation reside inside the IBA. We will either see cable become the responsibility of the IBA or we will see this new regulatory body drawing upon IBA staff.

'These people at the IBA are the only ones in the country who have developed that peculiar genius for encouraging enterpreneurs while keeping the standard of content high. . . And we have, now, the experience of AM television and the Fourth Channel. So I think we're well placed to do the job.'

Lord Thomson's IBA might be well placed to provide foot soldiers at the barricades against the Visigoths. But the notion of the particularly suspicious species, the 'entrepreneur', being encouraged was enough to get George Howard, Chairman of the BBC, going for his handkerchief.

The BBC has been nervous about the whole idea of 'communication' for many years. Constructed as a 'cultural civil service', it saw itself at the centre of the development of media in the United Kingdom. Howard spoke in measured tones, occasionally pausing to wipe a perspiring dome, modulating the voice of reason to puncture the bombast's balloon of the Atlanta cowboy.

'The BBC has noted before that some of the initial euphoria about cable might be misplaced,' he said. 'We question if people may be putting the cart before the horse. Many point to the American experience. They speak of the 'cool breeze of freedom' which has brought deregulation, and with it a healthy atmosphere where the private sector may lay cables and develop all aspects of the media. But this is not so. The regulatory agency there, the Federal Communications Commission, has more than 200 pages of rules and regulations for cable and there are, in addition, the many rules laid down by the city councils. 'And to those who look to the private sector leaping in with both feet I might quote from the American business maga-zine Baron's Weekly. *They say the cable market is now judged 'iffy' by the stock market. It just might be a bubble ready to burst. The people in the City might want to think about that.*

'Now I think it must be clear that in this country the deregulators want to make money. They are not particularly interested in the balanced presenta-tion of programmes to the whole British population. Quite apart from the damage this might do to the creative side of the industry, it could break down the traditional structure of British broadcasting which, everyone agrees, is not what we want to see. Privately developed cable will never reach everyone in the country. If you live in the countryside you'll never get it. Poorer inner city areas will go to the bottom of the list. There is a great danger that a cable television system could accentuate and aggravate social disparities. It would be ultimately devisive.

'Now this is not the case with direct broadcasting from satellite. It is quite straightforward. It will be universally available from the outset. If people want to equip themselves with a receiving dish they will get the programmes. (See background note 1.) But if we allow Pay-TV to pro-liferate I'm worried we'll see a tower of Babel instead of a new revolution. We should proceed in a regulated framework. I, for one, would be happy to see the IBA take up this role.'

It was a traditional presentation. Evil was represented by a cable industry given over to the private sector. These people, known to have only one aesthetic – profit – might be depended upon to create inequalities in the way they allowed cable systems to evolve. The BBC, on the other hand, with heavy investments in satellite TV systems, was pushing direct satel-lite broadcasting. Even so, George Howard still managed to portray the 'democratic' satellite television technology without explaining how a dish aerial must be in line of sight of the satellite. This immediately counts out a large proportion of British city dwellers. Cables would still be necessary to deliver satellite programmes.

But there was something else happening at Edinburgh which went much deeper than technological choice. During previous 'periods of tran-sition' the line-up had been the government and its advisers in public broadcasting and the civil service, holding the dam against the uncertain-ties of media mixed with private capital. Now that traditional alliance was in pieces. The person making George Howard and Lord Thomson ner-

128

vous was the Minister of Technology himself, Kenneth Baker, and the festival audience was treated to a rare sight. The government, taking its lead from the private communications sector, was calling for a speedy move into the information age.

Tory Visions: a New Information Industry?

Since the Conservative government took office in 1979, a veritable landslide of Cabinet-level decisions have put information technology at the centre of public policy initiatives. Kenneth Baker and his ministerial colleagues see broadcasting as simply one sector about to be affected. But if the Edinburgh 'insiders' were only talking about how to regulate these services, not questioning the existence of cable and satellite, that was good enough.

For the Conservatives the key to overhauling the British economy rests with private industry. If industry is to be given the chance to do its work its must be provided with incentives, and one way of offering incentive is to free certain areas from what is called 'the dead hands of state bureaucracy'. This is complicated when those areas being freed have 'entrenched' or 'well established' financial structures, production expectations, worker/management relations, market monopolies and trade unions. But it is *uncomplicated* when the industry does not yet wholly exist. It requires only legislation and if the legislation can be got into place fast enough, private industry can have its head. New companies will spring up. Jobs will be created while the infrastructure is being constructed and the feverish activities of new companies competing for supremacy in a new industry can be used by the government to show how a policy of letting private industry have the 'freedom' to operate creates a bustling economy, offering more jobs. With this connection established in the public mind the government can then push forward with the idea that privatisation is the best way to get other state-owned industries bustling.

But the incentives must come first. During March 1982 the British government therefore delivered a two-pronged assault aimed at opening wide the 'information industry' and laying the foundation for a new communications system. Firstly, Home Secretary William Whitelaw announced a programme for 'direct broadcasting by satellite'. A satellite system would be built, launched and operating by 1986. The BBC would have two channels. They would derive revenue from licence fees and subscription sales throughout Europe. They would be no experimental period. To allow this, said Whitelaw, would be to allow British industry to fall behind others in the same field.

Importantly, Whitelaw, whose Ministry is responsible for broadcasting – including the BBC, IBA and small cable subscription television experiment (see below) – did not justify this move in terms of cultural development. Taking a lead from the Departments of Industry and Trade, he spoke of an important stimulation to industry to create jobs and increase exports. Two weeks later, the Information Technology Advisory Panel (ITAP) released a report entitled 'Cable Systems'. The Panel – six men all drawn from private companies with a vested interest in the proliferation of computer/data systems (see background note 2) – had been formed in July 1981 to advise the Cabinet on the best means of developing information technologies. They were also assisted by the Information Technology Unit, a group of civil servants attached to the Cabinet office.

Their report said in essence that a 30-channel cable system had to be laid as fast as possible. These men had no experience or expertise in telecommunications or broadcasting, but they didn't beat about the bush: 'We believe cable to be an essential component of future communications systems, offering great opportunities for new forms of entrepreneurial activity, and substantial direct and indirect industrial benefits. However, the initial financing of cable systems will depend upon none of these things, but upon estimates of the revenue from additional popular programming channels . . . cable systems will go through an initial phase when their attraction will be based on 'entertainment' considerations. Private sector finance is available for investment in cable systems – there need be no call on public funds. . . The Government should announce, by mid-1982, the broad outlines of its future policy towards cable systems, in order to allow the private sector to start planning. . .'[1]

So the message to the government was clear: computer-communications could be very profitable for private industry. However, if a national cable system were to be made profitable in the short term it must be done with 'entertainment', the stock in trade of broadcasters. But ITAP was interested, in the long term, in information technologies (data systems, etc.). To sort out the 'loss leader' role to be played by broadcasters, a former Cabinet Secretary, Lord Hunt, was given a commission and told to go away for a few months, collect evidence, and come back before the end of 1982 with an outline for a national cable broadcasting system (see background note 5). Kenneth Baker put it this way: 'But after Hunt I think we should move quickly. Remember, it will take a year to eighteen months at least just to work out the technical details. I have several committees inside the ministry moving towards setting the required technical standards. To launch an experimental programme would probably set us back four or five years. We think there are hardware and software possibilities that make it useful for us to proceed towards a national system immediately. This is important because the money will depend on the city. There will not be a quick profit in this. It will pay back over a few years. We expect the city to proceed cautiously, doing their own research. We should be providing the right go-ahead atmosphere allowing them to get on with the job. Of course we must have some sort of regulation. However, to hold back the cable process because it might not reach everyone in the country right away is really holding back progress. Research has shown that people will find the money to pay for extra services if they want them. And, at any rate, I am an optimist. I believe that we will have the whole nation cabled from Land's End to John O'Groats within ten years. Regulations can see to that without reducing the investment potential for the private sector. Here we can look towards Canada and the work of their CRTC.'

One Canadian programme-maker observing the Edinburgh event greeted this innocent assertion with a wry smile. 'They have a lot to learn if they are able to copy the dismal performance of the CRTC in Canada,' he said (see Chapter 2). 'I think the real issue at stake here is not whether or not to have cable, satellite broadcasting or any other kind of new communications. If that were the debate they'd be looking harder at video cassettes, which have taken off here as they have not done in the

United States. When talking about programming it's all about the right sort of delivery system to fit the predilections of the national culture. People here are obviously going for video cassettes. But what these Commissions are really saying is that the government wants to deregulate the whole economy, and they're using cables as the cutting edge of that campaign in the communications sector.'

People already have one of the best television systems in the world here, content wise. In North America people have gone for alternative delivery systems because they offer an alternative to a mediocre advertising-dominated television industry. If you listen to the financial people, they are still trying to figure out how to make a profit out of cabling-up Britain. In North America they reckon enough people are willing to pay to get better television that they can afford to lay the fibre optics that will bring in the interactive information services at a later date which could really pay off.

Here, there doesn't seem to be that entertainment incentive. That means the market for cable will be amongst the sector of society which demands data/information capabilities now. That is the business community. This might extend to residential areas where incomes allow people to hook on to a business-oriented cable service that is passing through their neighbourhood. But that means your cable system is going to be a piecemeal affair unless the government takes it over.

At least two groups agree with this Canadian estimation: the people backing the cable television experiment licensed by the Home Office in 1980, and the financial backers for Britain's first private telecommunication system, Mercury.

British Cable TV: the first experiments

'The experience with a single channel movie service on cable is, you know, not a barn burner, it's not a disaster. The lessons are that we have to get better at a lot of things we're doing now – improve the service, improve the marketing – and we also have to look toward a lot more new services if we're going to have a viable cable communications system.' That was the opinion of Richard Thorn, brought in from the heart of cable country in Pennsylvania, to run Thorn-EMI's Cinematel cable television experiment. It had been running little short of a year when Thorn spoke up at the Television Festival in Edinburgh. His company was one of seven licensed to carry a single channel of movies by the Home Office during a two-year experiment.

Before ITAP changed the government's attitude and pace on cable, William Whitelaw gave a perk to an old lobby, the Cable Television Association of Great Britain. This trade body represents the commercial companies which feed television signals on cables to eight per cent of Britain's TV households (a further five per cent are serviced on British Telecom cables). Led by the giant in the field, Rediffusion, these companies had been complaining bitterly for ten years that the licence they receive limits them to a relay of authorised (already existing) radio and television signals. There was no money in this.

At the beginning of the 1970s the then controlling body, the Ministry of Post and Telecommunications, issued licences to give companies for local 'community programmes'. The 'experiment' was initiated by a Conservative government. Commercial cable companies took it as a signal that cable services were about to be allowed on a scale equal to North America. Investors flocked across the Atlantic, many from Canada where a cable free-for-all had just been slowed down by government control, forcing capital to look to other 'open' markets.

But half-way through the planned three years 'first stage', Labour returned to power. The government made it clear there was no intention to allow 'commercial' programming, and the cable companies, who had been bearing the cost of the 'community' programmes, considering it part of the capitalisation for future commercial services, returned to relay operations.

Not everyone went home empty-handed. The 'experiment' sparked an interest in community television. It was a short-lived phenomenon, a figment of the apolitical 'alternative' movement prevalent at the time. As Peter Lewis put it in his report on community television for the British Film Institute in 1978: 'The advocates of community television have indeed so far failed to find a long-term solution to the problem of finance. . . There is, however, evidence of the success of community television in satisfying local needs . . . those working in community television saw their job as providing something different, using an approach that differed markedly from that of broadcasting professionals. The approach involved putting the local community (or its constituent 'communities of interest') first, rather than the dictates of a mass, scheduling or artistic or professional excellence.[2]

Notwithstanding this important early brush with television by those of 'alternative' persuasion, the commercial companies became hardened to their image of grasping freebooters. They expected nothing from Labour and got it. But as soon as decently possible after the 1979 election William Whitelaw told the Cable Television Association that its members would get the break they had long awaited. The proviso was that no foreign, particularly American, capital be obviously behind the companies. This rule was not difficult to comply with. Most of the North Americans had drifted away during the drought years. When it came to the test only one company, Wellingborough Cablevision, had Canadian money. For the sake of propriety it was not allowed an experimental licence.

The 'cable experiment' was announced to the House of Commons in November 1980. It would be a feature film service: existing cable subscribers in 'test' areas would be offered a slab of films every evening on a channel separate from those normally used to relay radio and television transmissions. Subscribers would pay a monthly fee. The licensees had to abide by existing British Board of Film Censors' regulations, show no X-rated films before 10.00 p.m. and wait 12 months before showing newly registered films. They would not be allowed exclusive rights to sporting events, were banned from carrying adverts and had to research response to the service for submission to the Home Office. So the experiment was by no means free of all strings. None was going to make a profit, least of all the programme suppliers who had to bargain with film distributors seeking rates equivalent to those paid by cinemas. (See background note 3.) Nicholas Mellersh, director of Rediffusion's Subscription Television Unit, felt it was a pretty poor Tory show after all those years of waiting. In the July 1981 issue of the Cable Television Association's *Journal*, he wrote:

'It is nearly three years since the then government's post-Annan White Paper agreed to the concept of pilot schemes. It is 18 months since the Home Secretary announced that he was actually prepared to licence pilot schemes. In the face of these delays it is quite remarkable that cable operators have not long since lost patience and decided that the future of their companies can be better assured in other areas of commercial activity not subject to the procrastinations of government. And what logical reason can there be for the licence conditions placed on cable operators. . . It is the product of private investment and there is no case for controls other than the law of the land . . . the long-term viability of premium services over cable will only occur when the dead hand of government restrictions is removed and the industry is allowed to develop like any other.' But a year later, in Edinburgh, Richard Thorn was more sanguine: 'In my personal opinion the Home Office rules are not onerous. They're not what's key about the pilot scheme. What is key about it is that they were pilot schemes in the first place. That is, they were set up in limited areas and they were set up for a limited time. They don't really have that much to do with cable. They just happen to be on cable. They are, in fact, more the first sort of toe-wetting of single-channel Pay-TV oriented towards feature films. They could be over the air as regular television. They could be coming from a satellite. They could be coming through the mail, I suppose, on video cassettes, I don't know. But at any rate it is important to remember it is a single-channel not a multi-channel environment that we're talking about.

'The Rediffusion marketing approach has been the best, bar none,' said Thorn, holding up a glossy brochure listing the latest films on offer from the company's 'starview' service. They've been rewarded with the highest penetration rate: 14 per cent of homes passed by Rediffusion cables in those cities are taking Starview. Take-up rates are half that for the other services.

'We can also compare that to similar subscription services in the United States and the rate of 'take-up' during initial periods is just about the same. But the service costs a lot more, when you compare incomes, here than in the US, and there is not as much cable on the ground. Therefore, it's difficult to see a single service of this kind bringing in any big revenues.

'So you cannot look at the pilot schemes as either vanguards of the media millenium or the advanced party of the barbarians at the gates. . . After all, the only reason for cable is that it's a very, very wide electronic highway that can do a very large number of things. Obviously, we're going to have to take advantage of that highway and develop a whole range of services adding up to the sort of composite revenue stream which will be needed to make it worthwhile.'

To anyone following the 1982 proceedings in Edinburgh closely, voice/ image synchronisation started to drift apart at about this point. Here was a man right inside the entertainment cable industry saying the only way companies like his were going to see a profit was to invest in 'a whole range of services'. What Thorn meant was interactive information systems for home and office, of which entertainment is one component. Yet the Minister, Kenneth Baker, was going round with an image drawn by ITAP. That had the private sector, the cable industry, rolling up its sleeves and getting out the cash to cable-up the nation for the short-term entertainment money-earner which would pay for the long-term wait until everyone started using interactive information services.

There were several different approaches to this apparent contradiction among those paddling the same boat. One group said that whether or not cable entertainment could find a market in this country was irrelevant. Satellite broadcasting would open up a vast European cable market. Revenues here could be very high indeed, more than enough to plough into a long-term wait.

Others said nothing could be drawn from the movie channel experiment. Real commercial cable television was 'narrow casting'. That meant programmes could be tailored to special interest groups, like the magazine industry. This would add up to more than enough revenue potential to draw private investment.

Still others thought that people taking an 'either-or' approach were just not beginning to grasp the truly revolutionary nature of the cable/satellite technology. The integration of electronic publishing, banking, shipping, home systems monitoring and entertainment would just be too much to pass up. As soon as they realised what was coming their way, British people would be queueing up to get on the cable. In the meantime, programme costs could be drastically reduced by simply getting away from the movie concept. Video technology was now so cheap and high quality that first-rate programmes could be made for a fraction of the current telefilm industry norm. Very few of the bored programme-makers bothering to attend these sessions seemed to understand that, in amongst the confusion of 'new technologies' and half-baked speculation drawn from chronic misinformation, their sub-industry was being sized up for an assault on wage/fee structures enabling a cost-effective entertainment sector to plan its loss-leader campaigns.

However, the nagging question left unasked was who exactly was going to lay the cables in the first place. Existing cables for television in Britain are primitive even by coaxial standards. Most can carry only one additional channel to the regular BBC/IBA stations. Because of this much depends on whether the government accepts the Hunt Commission proposal that cable companies must carry existing stations; short-term profitability could turn on this alone. But everyone agrees that the minimum number of channels needed to ensure growth towards an interactive system is 30. This calls for a major technological investment. Who is going to pay for it if the government isn't? Who needs it now?

Mercury: the first private telecom network

The Cable and Wireless company does not, as its name suggests, make telecommunications equipment. Yet it is one of the most lucrative telecommunications shares on the London Stock Market. Instead, it supplies management services to governments which want their telecommunications systems to operate efficiently. The Cable and Wireless franchise to run the Hong Kong system alone accounted for 60 per cent of the company's £62.6 million 1980 pre-tax profits. The rest was provided by other 'non-franchise' contracts, like the supply of a communications system to the Saudi Arabian National Guard. The firm also runs four subsidiaries in the United States selling 'enhanced' phone equipment, a loss-making franchise in the Yemen Arab Republic, and has a fresh contract to run the Macau telecommunications system. (See background note 4.)

Until October 1981, Cable and Wireless was a wholly state-owned company. A little less than half the equity was then sold to private share buyers. The deal brought in £189 million for the government. Cable and Wireless Chairman Eric Sharp said at the time that the company needed to be free of the Treasury if it were to continue growing and moving into new markets. The Treasury treated Cable and Wireless like 'a fifth wheel on a stagecoach,' said Sharp. It was 'not particularly technically competent to judge projects'. The project which has now brought this shadowy management services group out of the colonial past and into the British information revolution is called Mercury.

When the government put the company's equity on the market it went with 'an agreement in principle' to allow Cable and Wireless, British Petroleum (BP) and Barclays Bank to finance, construct and operate a private telecommunications network. Phase one of the project envisaged a 700-mile loop of optical fibre cables linking seven English cities. The cables would be laid along British Rail tracks. Microwave radio would be used to transmit signals between the loop and aerials installed on tall buildings in city centres. Communications would then be relayed to individual users by 'cellular radio'.

The Mercury consortium was granted its licence by the end of 1981, and in July 1981, and in July 1982 announced that Sir Michael Edwardes, retiring Chairman of British Leyland, would take a two-day-a-week Chairmanship. His job was to 'get a better deal from the government'. The reason for this was that Mercury would have to use British Telecom lines to switch subscriber voice/data calls overseas. But British Telecom, anxious to maintain its monopoly position was playing hard to get. Its position had changed drastically in the 18 months up to July 1982 and looked like changing again; Mercury's attitude was like rubbing salt in the wounds.

Off the record, Mercury personnel made no bones about their intended market. This was the very largest corporations and that financial nexus located in the City of London. The corporations wanted to talk amongst themselves, communicate instantaneously with their subsidiaries, and link efficiently with data banks whenever required. But this called for a 'phone system which is 'lean and responsive'. Many corporate communications planners had despaired of finding this trait in the government 'phone service long ago. As one critic put it, 'There is a growing demand for digital services, particularly among business subscribers. BT has not shown it can react quickly in this area. It's plagued by bureaucratic inertia, ossified industrial relations and financial restraints. They have the engineering expertise and the equipment, but they don't know how to serve the market.'

While Michael Edwardes was signing up, Mercury announced that its London services would go into operation in March 1983. There was a keen demand for the system, so much so that an eighth city, Preston, would be added to the loop, demanding an extra 150 miles of optical fibre cable. The entire system would go into operation some time in 1984. It would carry 8,000 simultaneous telephone conversations or an equivalent volume of data communications as well as two-way televised video conferencing.

This is the image that the ITAP and Kenneth Baker have been carrying around. The system will reach the most lucrative urban markets with the highest density of organisations capable of paying the subscriptions to make a private cable system work. Mercury/Cable and Wireless projections use the system taking a portion of the 'new cable market' equal to one per cent of British Telecom's revenue, about £40 million in 1980. As time goes by, Mercury predicts circuits will be leased to third parties interested in operating 'value added' services: these include access to data networks and viewdata information banks. And those lucky enough to live near some London or provincial corporate office will have the cable/information revolution close at hand.

Of course, the 'cable information revolution' has already made one pass at the British public. There were few takers. British Telecom thought that Prestel would take the nation into the future. 'From the bottom up'. The viewdata information service would bypass that now traditional trickle-down structure whereby innovations handled by the private sector move from the business sector towards the people.

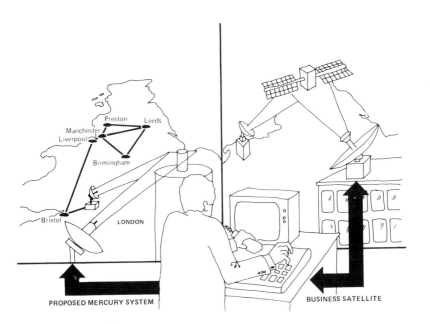

The proposed business network, the Mercury System, using fibre optic cables for traffic domestically in the UK and satellites for the international transmission of voice and data information.

Edinburgh, July 1979. The envelope arrived at the wrong address. Or at least the computer hadn't processed the change of address sent out by another computer on behalf of the travel agent's office. So the invitation to view Prestel fell into the hands of two journalists sitting in their basement looking for an afternoon freebee.

On their way to the post office building in central Edinburgh one explained how he got into journalism via computers. 'Abstracting is an exacting skill. We were doing it for a journal of agricultural science which went all over the Commonwealth. Subscribers got their journal of abstracts and the added advantage of having the whole collected series of journals put on to a data base. The process was rather easy. We simply keyboarded the abstract. The punched tapes were used for typesetting. They were also used to transmit the abstracts to the database, which was located in the United States.

The database itself was primed to allow searching through certain keywords. You could do quite creative searching because you could get the full abstract out of the system. This also called for some rather creative abstracting. You would have to think in terms of the person looking through the database as well as reading the hard copy. The database had to be consistent. If a name or technical term was spelt wrong just once the computer would miss it. Today there are full text services with very fast key word indexes that allow you to "get in and get out" very quickly indeed. But these are relatively recent. For years it was rather expensive, because our abstracts, for example, went on to the Lockheed Dialog system in California. It paid to be quick. Just as I was leaving they were negotiating to go on to Euronet-DIANE. But there were all sorts of problems with that one. It seems the European computers couldn't speak the same communications language as the British ones, or something. No one was ready to budge. Typical of a bureaucratic organisation where every nation has a vested interest. Nevertheless, the European network would be cheaper than going on line to America.

But I really don't know where Prestel is going to fit in. The scientific and technical networks have been set up for a while and I don't think anyone is going to crack that game. If anything the cost of transmission will come down so much the Lockheed types will soon be offering full text services. One service, Nexis, has been doing full text for a while. They specialise in political and economic news (see Box on 'Electronic Publishing').

I suppose it has a convenience factor because of operating through an ordinary television. But it really depends what is put on it. No one from the scientific and technical community needs it. Businesses on the lookout for an on-line service have had a few years of private networks offering data and information. And, of course, there are the mini- and micro-computers with all those programmes tailored to every business need.

As for the general public, if they're asking you to charge it all up on your phone bill I just don't see it catching on. People are still treating the phone as a luxury. They don't see it as a tap that gets turned on whenever the urge strikes. It's expensive. But as far as I can see the Prestel people have to find a mass audience if they are going to make the thing pay. This little presentation is going to be interesting.'

At the door, the Prestel representative was unctuously welcoming. He didn't look like a born salesman and, as it turned out, he wasn't. 'What we'd like to do today, ladies and gentlemen, is give you a little demonstra-

tion of a new and, I might say, rather revolutionary technology. If you'll just watch the screen we'll turn down the lights.'

Electronic Publishing and Databases

The most sophisticated database on offer in Britain is NEXIS. This was developed by the Mead Corporation (an American paper giant listed in the Fortune 500) and is marketed in this country by Butterworth's Telepublishing (owned by IPC).

It searches full text on any word in the text with the exception of common words like 'and', 'if' or 'not'. The NEXIS database holds full text of a wide variety of publications specialising in politics and economics; among others it includes *The American Banker*, the *Washington Post*, *The Economist*, *Christian Science Monitor*, the BBC's monitoring service, the Chinese national news agency, Latin American Newsletters and two of the biggest Japanese wire services.

So let's imagine you want to research a cable TV project. You ask for the Number of entries in *The Economist* using the words CABLE TV. This will generate say 2,000 entries. You could at this point look through all 2,000 references. Each reference gives a headline, a sub-headline, the author where applicable and the number of words in the article.

So if you want to refine your search you might ask for CABLE TV AND LONDON. This will generate those articles which have both these key words within ten lines of each other. This will probably reduce your search to say, 120 entries. From here you might refine the search even further by adding other levels of search, adding other key words. By this stage you probably have 15 references and you can either examine these on-screen or get them printed out.

NEXIS developed from LEXIS which offers a similar service for all legal cases. The company has just over 1,000 customers in the UK. Other databases in the UK fall into two broad categories; financial and scientific. There is a whole cluster of financial services including Fintel, Reuters and Finsbury Data Service's Textline.

The latter was set up by British and Commonwealth Shipping and a group of financial institutions. Based on a Hewlett Packard mini-computer, it provides abstracts of all the main financial publications. It has easy-to-use software (similar to NEXIS) which searches by words or combinations of words. There are few users outside the City of London and the company is not yet showing a profit.

The largest and oldest database is Lockheed Dialog. It provides mainly abstracts of scientific journals and is much favoured by research departments in companies and academic libraries. It is slightly cheaper to use than NEXIS but it only has abstracts; these suffer, like indexes, from the priorities and quirks of the individual who designs the system. It has about 1,200 subscribers worldwide.

There is a welter of scientific and economic databases under the umbrella of Euronet-Diane. It plays a significant role in the EEC debate on information flows.

Finally, Robert Maxwell's Pergammon has acquired a company called Infoline which observers believe he will use to construct and market a database of his scientific and learned journals.

Electronic publishing differs from databases in that it is used primarily as a source of 'instant' information like a newspaper. A US company called Newsnet will shortly be available in the UK offering a wide range of specialist newsletters available shortly after their publication date using a wide range of cheap micro-computers.

Electronic publishing has three distinct advantages over print:
1 Its speed. A subscriber can read what has been written probably less than two hours after you've finished writing it. It can provide a specialised electronic news service for users. It could offer anything from information on a demonstration called at short notice to a news service on energy price developments. It can also provide instant commentary on events.
2 It can be easily searched and indexed. With existing software, you can create indexes to material, search full-text on key words or scan headlines only. If the NCCL want as much information as possible to prepare a case on official secrets, it scans the relevant magazines and checks them through.
3 In the jargon, it is 'inter-active'. With a properly designed system, the publisher can receive information or queries from its subscribers. With a printer attached, you could receive papers in advance of a conference. You could circulate articles or motions for comments.

Development of this kind of electronic publishing will speed up over the next five years. It depends on three things:
☐ The falling price of micros. These are now between £300–£1,000 and are continuing to fall in price. Following a similar growth rate to video machines, the number of home computers is probably now well over the million mark. It's a cheaper way of getting electronic publishing and databases than Prestel or cable TV.
☐ Early in 1983 British Telecom will launch Telecom Gold, an electronic mail service. Using a service developed by a company called Dialcom, it acts as an electronic mailbox. You can put up an issue of your electronic publication and only those subscribers with the right password can access it.
☐ Increasingly, publications will be set on typesetting machines that generate floppy discs or magnetic tapes. Already Linotype Paul are selling a modified Apple micro-computer which will give you a floppy disc. This disc provides all the instructions to the Linotron 202 typesetter to give you fully typeset copy. Because the article is stored electronically, it can be proof-read several times even before it's set, using the VDU, or a paper

print-out. This will mean that publishers will be able to use their electronic version of their typeset copy (probably set in-house) to sell electronically.

What followed was a piece of video advertising. It told how the information retrieval system had been brought out of Post Office laboratories in 1974 by Sam Fedida and a group of technologists in response to a felt need for some means of tracking down available rooms in a city full of hotels. The film went on to show how the Prestel concept had grown to include a regular television set linked to a minicomputer storing 'pages' of information. The Post Office had made a 'bold decision'. There would be no test period. The Prestel revolution would be brought to the public immediately. So now, in 1979, well ahead of similar systems being tested around the world, the British public would have the opportunity to get in on the information revolution.

Already computers were in place designed to hold up to 250,000 pages of information. Local computers would store the most 'popular' types of information locally (railway timetables, newspapers, local events updates) and less frequently used pages would remain in a central 'warehouse', which could be called up in a second or two. So far only one

Buying a home using Prestel.

regional computer existed, in London, but there were plans for computers in Birmingham, Manchester and Edinburgh.

Response from 'information providers' had been encouraging. Already 150 publishing and other organisations were asking to lease pages, and there was a waiting list. The Post Office itself would take no editorial control of information, beyond basic laws of copyright and common decency. The user would pay three charges: a local telephone charge for the period of connection, a charge for the time actually 'logged on' to Prestel, and charges, if any, levied on each 'page' by the information provider. At that time a typical 'logging' charge was set at two pence.

The lights went up and there was a buzz of excitement. The assembled travel agents thought the idea showed promise. 'Here's a problem,' said one. 'Do you mean that every time we hook up it ties up our phone line?', 'Yes' was the answer. 'What if we're already linked to one of the private airline travel services?' said another. 'The advantage of this system is that you have access to the full range of travel options,' said a member of the Prestel sales team.

The agents crowded to the front round one of the Prestel sets. A sweating engineer was attempting to show the search system. The 'line' kept going down. 'You have to understand we have to wait for a line to the London computer for each separate call. All the bugs aren't out yet. When we get the Edinburgh computer up and running things will be easier.'

'It's a bit of a mess,' muttered the science journalist. 'The search system is very complicated. It's a tree system and you have to go right through every indexed possibility before you come anywhere near the page you're after. That will certainly cost a lot. I doubt the average person with a phone will jump at it.'

Later, at a tea and biscuits gathering after the demonstration, a Prestel executive expressed his own doubts: 'I really couldn't say how it's going to go. Everything has happened so fast. Up until six months ago I was in engineering. They transferred me and I've had to do a crash course. The simple fact is that we don't have a large sales staff. We've never had to sell anything. Telephones are just there, a public facility. You either have one or you don't. The notion of going out on the doorstep to actually sell these things is completely new to everyone here. Of course there are the marketing and advertising consultancies. But they're not allowed to sell anything. It's in the union agreement. When the engineering union saw Prestel coming they got a contract which said no new staff could be brought in on this if there were engineers in danger of being made redundant. Well, there have been cutbacks, so a lot of us have been turned into Prestel 'demonstrators and salesmen'. 'That's typical,' said the science journalist strolling back to his office. 'They've got a revolutionary technology, a contract which says they can't bring in experienced sales people, and absolutely no experience of mass marketing. If you ask me, it's going nowhere. A few travel agents and small businesses may use it, but it's so difficult to get extra phone lines the trouble will probably put people off. How long did it take us to get our phone? Three months? And that was with lots of complaining. They've just never had to hustle, as the Americans say. If I was in business I'd look for a private line computer package tailored to my own purposes.'

Prestel goes back to business

In July 1982 IPC (International Publishing Corporation) threw in the towel. On page three of the company's journal, *Viewdata and TV User* (*including the official Prestel Directory*) it was announced that the organisation was being sold to Eastern Counties Newspaper Group to be merged with the quarterly *Prestel User*. The terse statement continued: 'The disposal of V & TVU by IPC Business Press follows quickly on the IPC decision to phase out its Prestel information-provider division, IPC Viewdata, by the end of August. IPC Executive Peter Yapp said that Prestel's development has been so slow and costs had reached such an unacceptably high level, that he could see "no light at the end of the tunnel" for the IPC operation. It was time to rethink the "information revolution for the masses".'

Everyone inside British Telecom was by then admitting that they'd made some big mistakes with the introduction of Prestel. They had hoped to be well on the way to the 'mass information market' by the end of 1980, with 50,000 units installed. In fact, there were only 13,000 in operation, mostly at businesses, not in homes. The major customers turned out to be in the travel and brokerage industries. These users wanted up-to-date information on everything from airline schedules to commodity prices. British Telecom analysts also believed that the slow response from television manufacturers had been a blow. A specially adapted set was required, but the makers have been hesitant about committing really substantial resources to an untested market.

Prestel's audience was re-assessed. A major national advertising campaign was launched in 1981 focusing on the 'narrow' business sector. A cost-cutting programme was put into place to reduce losses, then running at about £4 million a quarter. Fourteen of the 20 regional computers were disconnected. One hundred staff were 'redeployed' throughout British Telecom and eight of Prestel's ten regional centres were closed.

In the spring of 1982 British Telecom introduced 'Gateway'. This allows 'private user networks' to function through Prestel, with information seekers able to access private databases housed somewhere outside Prestel's own computer. This additional service, it was hoped, would allow Prestel to compete with existing and future data networks. Gateway is also seen as a 'currency transaction service' with British Telecom trying to interest American Express and Barclays Bank. Finally, Gateway allows people who buy micro-computers to 'plug in' to the phone lines.

In effect, British Telecom has turned the original Prestel into a digital communications system similar to those private services on offer in North America. British Telecom has tried to present this as a positive and realistic move. It was, in fact, both a reaction to a mass marketing failure and part of a broader re-alignment within the state monopoly. For by the time British Telecom launched the new-look Prestel, the telecommunications world had changed a great deal.

British Telecom for sale

In 1980 the Conservative government had separated the Post Office from telecommunications, calling the new organisation British Telecom (BT). The 1981 Telecommunications Act further opened out the telecommunications monopoly and specified a three-year period of 'slowly increasing involvement from the private sector'. By the summer of 1981 the government was calling for the wholesale de-nationalisation of BT, with the sale of 50 per cent of the company to the private sector through the stock market.

The attack on British Telecom's monopoly started with a report written by Professor Michael Beesley of the London School of Business for the then Minister of Industry, Sir Keith Joseph, in 1981. Beesley said starkly that British Telecom had no right to a total monopoly of telecommunications. Private companies should be allowed to lease line from British Telecom to provide value added services. He also recommended the licensing of rival telecommunications systems, connection of 'third party' equipment to British Telecom lines and the contracting out of maintenance on Post Office telephone lines.

BT responded with its own man, a Cambridge academic called Brian Reddaway. According to Reddaway, rates would go up and the number of new subscribers coming on to the system would go down. For a country with one of the lowest numbered subscribers in the industrial world (60 per cent of households have telephones) this was not a useful tactic. Reddaway also noted that British Telecom gained most of its profits from long-distance and City of London lines. Any private companies entering the field would go for these lucrative areas, creaming off revenues which had been subsidising the rest of the system.

Up to this point the slow-moving engineering section had used its contracting system to encourage British companies in the field. Stiff competition in high revenue areas would force BT to get new equipment as fast as it came on to the market, whether or not it was British. Reddaway concluded that the whole prospect of handing part of the industry over to the private sector could mean 'serious under-utilisation of BT assets, greatly reduced BT investment and employment'. Undeterred, the Conservative government's Telecommunications Act came into force on October 1, 1981, putting on the statute book most of what Beesley had called for.

Less than a year later the Mercury private telecommunications system was starting to lay fibre optic cable around the country. At the same time, a wide variety of equipment, including modems, private branch exchanges and value added networks were selling briskly, often in advance of getting BT approval. This technical seal of approval provided BT with an ideal delaying device to fight a rearguard battle while positioning itself for a completely 'open' telephone market in 1984.

Whichever way you look at it, something had to give. BT was in the fastest growing area of the economy with one of the slowest moving organisations in Europe. Arthur Moffat is a publisher in Edinburgh with a long, sad story to tell about the national phone service. He is a staunch Labour man with co-operative leanings. He's ready to give every nationalised company the benefit of the doubt, but his patience has been slowly eroded by his dealings with BT.

'The last time I was working in London was horrific. We had three telex lines out of the country. There were periods when the 'lines would go down' almost every day, sometimes for three hours. That does not make for efficient information organisation. After a while it really was no use calling the engineers. They always said the same thing, and would make a note in their log book. Sometimes someone came to fiddle with the connection at our

building and other times they said they were dealing with it at the exchange.

'*During that time we were expanding and publishing a series of business newsletters for overseas consumption. We needed phone lines. As computer data networks started putting political and economic news on data bases we wanted to subscribe to them. For this we needed a modem and another phone line. But the average wait for a phone line was running between six and ten weeks. It was almost impossible to get a modem. Everyone acted as if they had never heard of it. We were asked to fill in a three-page questionnaire on fuzzy, duplicated paper. Nothing happened. After months of patient negotiation we had to write to a few MPs and pull some other strings.*

'*It reminds me of when I was out in Zambia. Everything provided by the government has to be 'paper-worked' in triplicate. The problem is the government hasn't got any forms! What they do is send out one sample form and then leave it up to the requesting agency to copy it by hand or find a rare duplicator to make up as many of these things as they need. When you think a whole sheaf of different forms is required every time one government worker in a rural hospital is paid you can see what kind of knot could build up.*

'*It seems to me that's what happened to the telephone system. They spent decades trying to produce the most efficient and durable phones in the world, and largely succeeded I think. They never had to sell anything. They never had to "please the consumer" or "react to business requirements".*'

'*But just because the organisation needs to be reformed to deal with new technologies and new kinds of demands on the phone system is no reason to join the Conservatives in a breathless backward rush to throw the whole thing into private hands. BT might be bad for some, for the specialist information industries in London and the corporate office needing lots of lines, but it still does provide a basic national service.*

'*Until it was threatened with privatisation it did try to bring its innovations to the mass of the people first, rather than special economic interest groups. You have to give them that much on Prestel. There are inefficiencies, and prices can be high. This calls for reform, not a wholesale endorsement of the American system.*

'*Of course I'm not saying Labour is any better. The pledge to re-nationalise the system in the hands of BT as soon as it returns to power is no help. We must redefine our own national priorities and arrange the services to suit. We could phrase the problem of BT in another way, and ask why successive governments have seen fit to centralise all the sections of industry requiring high levels of information in one part of the country, radiating out from central London. I'm sure a positive policy to decentralise these industries would not only provide jobs in our black spots but also make full use of the telecommunications system.*'

The privatized road to ruin?

When Chancellor of the Exchequer Sir Geoffrey Howe spoke to the Selsdon Group during the first week of July 1981 he imparted a rare bit of insight. The Group traditionally have an annual address which deals with the more theoretical aspects of the state of the economy. Sir Geoffrey's subject was the public utilities which he characterised as inefficient bureaucracies hopelessly compromised because their administration was smack in the middle of the government's political spider's web.

The only way these companies could be got to work properly, Sir Geoffrey opined, was to separate them from the government. They needed a dose of corporate logic. But they should first be divided into two groups: those in the public sector 'by accident', and those which could be considered 'natural monopolies'. Into the first group fell British Steel, British Airways, British Aerospace, National Freight Carriers, British Shipbuilders and British Leyland. Profitable companies in this group should go back to the private sector as soon as possible. Unprofitable ones needed to be 'scheduled for some future arrangement' so that public refinancing could be undertaken in the long-term hope of getting a return on investment.

For the second group – Gas, Electricity and Telecommunications – there were a number of options. The most obvious is the 'North American' option: separation from the government by partial or complete privatisation, with a Public Regulatory Body to monitor, negotiate and fix price structures so that the monopoly does not become abusive. Another possibility is regionalisation. This entails 'parcelling out,' say the electricity authorities, into virtually independent 'local private utilities' linked to the central agency in the same way that part-owned subsidiaries relate to 'corporate headquarters'. Of course, the best possible development would be a total change in the economic or technological foundation upon which a utility has risen to monopoly power. In that instance the government simply dissolves the monopoly, appoints a regulatory body, and sits back while the new market forces corporate efficiencies upon the old utility. It's a gift.

The reason why Sir Geoffrey Howe is sanguine about this last possibility is because he and the Conservative government believe that today's private corporation has evolved as the best way of conducting the affairs of society. Corporations in the electronics field, particularly computer-communications companies, so the logic goes, have come through the American international market of hard competitive knocks as survivors. They deserve respect and emulation.

The United Kingdom has been one of the most welcoming of nations to United States capital since the Second World War. The Americans chose Britain to operate from before they got the hang of the Euromarket towards the end of the 1960s. Nevertheless, US investment in the UK has continued to hover at around half of all American money in the EEC. The American way of doing business, therefore, has had a powerful impression on Britain.

As the corporate economies of scale bit off chunks of the UK economy the first reaction was to merge to meet the threat, thus pooling capital and production capabilities. The peak came in 1967–68. Five thousand British companies were involved in one way or another. In this period as well the Labour government-inspired Industrial Reorganisation Corporation (IRC) started arranging mergers by throwing finance into the hands of 'designated instruments'. General Electric and International Computers Limited (ICL) were born into their present form by this process.

Throughout the 1970s this process continued, especially while many of the internationalised companies made the difficult transition from the British Commonwealth to the EEC. It has been a hard trail. Very few British electronics firms remain intact. Only seven – General Electric, Racal Electronics, Plessey, Cable and Wireless, Thorn EMI, Standard Telephone and Cables and Ferranti – have continued in the list of Britain's largest 100 corporations. ICL, for example, the 'chosen instrument' for the computer industry, has been forced to make a series of agreements to market Fujitsu mainframe computers. In all sectors of computer sales IBM towers over the competition. This is despite a 'positive action' policy by many central and regional government offices to use ICL equipment.

In one important area British firms *are* surviving nicely: 'personal' micro-computers, In the middle of July 1982 Sinclair Research was leading all other makers with its under £50 micro. It was being used by schools, professionals preparing to use large machines in their daily work, and was recommended by Prestel. This is an exception. In most areas the toughening experience of the American corporate free market has simply relegated British companies to the backseat.

The private computer-communications sector, if not mimicking a style set by United States capital, is conceiving the information revolution in an American format. That format has very little to do with the 'invasion of US television culture', although it can't be discounted. It has a lot to do with the structuring of the relationship between a people, their culture and their economy. The new communications technologies in themselves are tools with the potential to advise and encourage changes in the relationship between culture and economy. But the tools can only work in a framework sympathetic to, and made by, people experiencing the changes. If this is not the case, people will get hurt. The tools will attack, wound, alienate, exploit and marginalise large sections of the population. In Britain this will mean worsening 'chronic' unemployment, degenerating health and educational standards, youth alienation, oppression of racial and sexual minorities, and intensification of conscious and unconscious exploitation of women. On the other hand, actual human economic life beyond food and materials production and manufacturing will revolve around the growing numbers needed in 'service' sectors to monitor and pacify the victims.

The danger of both the 'privatisation' and the 'nationalisation' models of the restructuring of industry as they now appear in Britain is that neither has any longer the assistance of people as its objective. They are stylistically opposed systems in and for themselves which use 'industries', 'sectors' and so on to settle old scores and pay old debts.

When they attempt to structure computer-communications in this way they are throwing long-established cultural and economic institutions at each other from new directions. The outcome cannot be foreseen.

'The problem is,' said trade union consultant Paul Willman, 'they're three or four steps ahead of us. When I was visiting the United States it was a real eye-opener. The printing industry there has been doing technology and efficiency research for years. When they introduce some new computerised systems the unions just don't know how to deal with it.

146

Now, that's the same as we have here.

'I suppose you could say that the print unions have been holding the line in London, but they haven't got effective forward research. They can't negotiate the future, only the past. We really have no one to blame but ourselves. The union movement is geared towards protecting what we have already. When you're thinking that way it's difficult to visualise new job descriptions, let alone a new way of living.

'But if I read these technological developments right, that is what we are going to have whether we like it or not. It will happen across the board, not just in this industry. Linking up all the unions in the printing and publishing trade is a first step. It's a step that should have been taken long ago. It doesn't solve the problem of how to deal with information systems, it only provides a united front that will always be seen as slowing things down until we come up with our own options.'

What those options will be depends upon the ability of the 'potential computer-communications victims' to realise their impending condition, centre their thoughts on the new information systems and articulate their vision of the culture/economy dynamic. Groups of 'potential victims' in other countries, notably France, have started this process. There has been no parallel development in Britain. Time is running out.

Footnotes

1. Information Technology Advisory Panel report, *Cable Systems*, HMSO, London 1982. Pages 7, 48, 50.
2. Peter Lewis, *Community Television and Cable in Britain*, British Film Institute, London 1978. Page 1. Anyone interested in the potential for likely 'access' channels for local authorities and other groups on Britain's new cable systems should read Andrew Bibby, Cathy Denford and Jenny Cross, *Local Television, Piped Dreams?* Redwing Press, Milton Keynes 1979.

Background notes

Background note 1
British Satellite Policy

On March 4 1982, following a commissioned Home Office report entitled 'Direct Broadcasting by Satellite' completed almost a year earlier, Home Secretary William Whitelaw announced a satellite policy. It has three main thrusts:

1. There will be a British satellite broadcasting system up to standards agreed at the 1977 World Administrative Radio Conference. The satellite used for this purpose will be built by British Aerospace.

2. In the first instance, the BBC will broadcast from the satellite. Other licensing arrangements will be made at a later date. The 'operator' of the satellite had yet to be designated, though this was expected to be United Satellites, a consortium bringing together British Aerospace, GEC-Marconi, British Telecom and the Rothschild Merchant Bank.

3. Two channels were allocated right away to the BBC. Others might be added later.

As the BBC geared up to offer DBS, a technical row broke out. The BBC was made to admit that the 'line of sight' requirements of dish aerials made the 'Direct' aspect of the broadcasting misleading. Most people would not be able to 'find' the satellite even if they could afford the aerials. Therefore, cable delivery of these programmes becomes an important factor.

Background note 2

The six members oof the Information Technology Advisory Panel were: Michael Aldrich (Managing Director, Rediffusion Computers); I. H. Cohen (Managing Director Mullard); C. A. Davies (Managing Director, Information Technology); D. F. Hartley (Director, Cambridge University Computing Services); C. N. Read (Director, Inter-bank Research Organisation); G. C. Southgate (Chief Executive, Computer Service Division, British Oxygen).

Background note 3

Existing UK commercial cable systems

Licensed operator	Programme supplier	Name of service	Location
Rediffusion	Rediffusion	Starview	Reading Pontypridd Hull Tunbridge Wells Burnley
Radio Rentals	Thorn-EMI Video Productions	Cinematel	Swindon Medway Towns (Chatham, Gillingham and Rochester)
British Telecom	SelecTV	SelecTV	Milton Keynes
Philips Cablevision	SelecTV	SelecTV	Tredegar Northampton
Visionhire Cable	BBC Enterprises	Showcable	London (various areas)
Cablevision	SelecTV	SelecTV	Wellingborough
Greenwich Cablevision	Greenwich Cablevision	Screentown	Greenwich

Source: John Howkins, *New Technologies, New Policies*, Broadcasting Research Unit, British Film Institute, London, 1982.

Background note 4

Cable & Wireless
Cable & Wireless manages the telecommunications systems of a number of Third World countries. These are:

Hong Kong
Philippines (external telecom services)
Macau
Cook Islands
Tonga
Solomon Islands
Fiji
Vanuatu
Bahrain
Yemen Arab Republic (external telecom services)
Qatar (external telecom services)
United Arab Emirates and Saudi Arabia (project management)
Gambia and Sierra Leone (external telecom services)
Botswana

Background note 5

The Hunt Report

In October 1982 the committee set up to investigate 'cable expansion and broadcasting policy' in Britain submitted its report to the government. Its chairman was Lord Hunt, a former top civil servant (Cabinet Secretary).

The report's main recommendations were:
1   Cable television should be developed without any restriction on the number of channels, the programmes broadcast or the charges made to customers.
2   Prospective cable operators – the managers of local cable services – would have to submit bids for a ten-year 'franchise' to a national cable authority. If successful, they would have a monopoly in their allotted area. The authority, the only regulating body, would have minimal powers of intervention in the running of cable companies.
3   BBC and ITV would be 'protected' by a rule that cable operators must carry all four existing channels on top of other programmes. The operators would also be expected to meet the same general standards of 'decency', etc., as BBC/ITV. The companies would be disallowed from gaining exclusive rights to major sporting events and, initially, from charging a special 'pay rate' for individual programmes.
4   Cable companies would make their money from rental, subscriptions for programmes and advertising.
5   The laying of cables would also be open to competitive bids, with cable operators able to lay cables as well.
6   Local and central government, as well as political parties, would be disbarred from participation in the ownership of cable companies.

The report described cable television as 'all about widening the viewers' choice'. It added, however, that 'at its best cable can help both business and the individual by providing new methods of working, buying and selling direct from the home. It could provide increased education and training in the home, and services such as electronic mail and telebanking, plus a greatly enriched choice of home entertainment. . . At its worst, it could lead to a waste of resources, risks to privacy and a lowering of the quality of broadcasting. . . '

There is little doubt that the Hunt Report went about as far along the road to deregulation as the government could have hoped for, and was immediately welcomed by prospective cable operators like Rediffusion. Predictions on the cost of a monthly cable rental ranged from £5 to £20. The *Daily Telegraph* described the cabling of 'urban Britain' as 'probably . . . the most important, and natural, industrial decision made by this present government'.

Glossary of technical terms

Cable Television
Cable television is already in operation throughout North America. In the United States the cable normally installed (coaxial) can deliver up to 50 television channels. Data/information transmission requires a narrower band width than television, so more of these services can be delivered on a single 'channel'.

Cable delivers in one of two ways – a 'trunk-tree' structure or a 'switched' structure. The first, and most widely used, operates like a tree, with a trunk and many branches. Signals are spread out along the system with the branches 'tapped' to serve each subscriber. The subscriber's cable receives all available signals on a continuous basis and the TV selector decides which will be pictured on the screen.

The switched system has a trunk and lines out toward groups of subscribers. All signals are marshalled at a switching box near communities of between 50 and 100 televisions. A smaller, cheaper coaxial cable is then run from the switching box to the individual televisions. When the subscriber makes a channel selection a signal runs to the switching box which returns the required channel service.

The tree system is the one favoured in America, but the switched system, developed in Britain, is recommended for areas which must 'cable-up' quickly to keep pace with information technologies. No matter which delivery structure is used, however, the trunk operates in the same way.

Chip/Micro-chip
A chip of silicon one-tenth the size of a postage stamp on to which the electronic circuitry of the computer is etched.

Coaxial Cable
A cable using a large number of different copper cables wrapped together in one large cable.

Copper-pair Cable
The oldest type of cable using twisted strands of copper. Very limited capacity for carrying information compared to the coaxial or fibre optic cable.

Direct Broadcasting Satellite/DBS
A satellite that enables television pictures and telephone conversations to be transmitted.

Fibre Optic Cable
It is made up of glass fibres and can carry as much as 500 times as many telephone conversations as the old copper wire system.

Hardware
The actual computer equipment and all the different bits of machinery you attach like printers, visual display units (VDUs) and disc drives.

LANs/Local Area Networks
A number of different computers with often very different functions (word processing, accounts, etc.) can be connected together in the same building and this is a Local Area Network.

Memory
This is the capacity the computer and its software have for recording information and the necessary instructions for manipulating the information. For micro-computers, this is stored on floppy discs which are put into disc drives. Memory is measured in bytes and you talk of a machine having say '10 megabytes of memory'. The programmer's skill lies in getting a great deal of information into as small a number of bytes as possible.

Micro-computer
This is a broad definition used to describe the latest generation of 8- or 16-bit computers. They are the product of increasing miniaturisation and dropping costs for computer

152

memory. Because they are relatively cheap they have an enormous number of applications from small businesses and professional organisations to the present generation of rather limited 'home' computers. They either operate with floppy discs (rather like an LP of tape-like material) or hard discs.

Micro-processors
A broad description of the type of silicon chip circuitry used in a wide range of things besides computers. For example, the latest generation of washing machines and stereos have micro-processors which control their operations.

Mini-computer
These were the first development down from the original mainframe computer. They operate with far larger amounts of memory than micros and their cost falls between the mainframe at the top end and the micro at the bottom end. As micros get more powerful, the dividing line between them and minis becomes very blurred.

Modem
This is the box which translates the information/data generated by a computer into a form so that it can be sent down the phone line. Another modem at the receiving end unscrambles the signals sent so that they reappear as sent on the receiving computer. When phone exchanges act as computers, there will no longer be any need for modems. You will be able to communicate computer to computer, direct. British Telecom in the UK controls the market for modems. You are not supposed to use any other modems except theirs. At present, these are cumbersome, expensive and old-fashioned.

Networks
As the word implies, this is a network of computers in several different locations (for example, the different subsidiaries of a manufacturing firm or a set of academic libraries) who are able to communicate with data from computer to computer. Recent advances mean that networks can now transmit voices. And with cable TV networks, you have the possibility of transmitting moving pictures. These networks can be transcontinental using satellites.

Pay-TV
The concept that you pay for specific programmes. The idea was rejected by the Hunt Report.

Printer
This enables you to print out information from the computer. There are three main types: Daisywheel (the slowest producing text like an electric typewriter); dot matrix (letters made up of lots of dots); laser (the largest printer type used for *Reader's Digest* type circulars).

Software
This is the part of the computer that makes it work. It enables the digital information to be stored and processed. You talk about a software programme and 'programming a computer' to do a task. Some of the programming is put into the machine's circuitry itself before it leaves the factory and some is loaded into the computer every time you switch on.

Telecommunications
A broad field covering all the different ways of transmitting voice and data, whether through cables or satellites.

Teletex
A generic term for sending text down the phone lines, a sort of electronic mail. It also includes facsimile transmission where a machine scans a piece of paper with text on it and reproduces in facsimile at the other end. This can be slow and the resulting copies vary in quality. Another problem is that there are several different standards used by various manufacturers which are not interchangeable.

VANs/Value Added Networks
These take two forms. You can rent telephone lines and connect up several different locations. Often big companies have their own internal phone systems connecting up several different offices. It can be used transcontinentally. For instance, Ford have their Detroit designers with a link to their designers in Europe. A private leased line is expensive initially but it doesn't matter how much you use it. Unlike a normal phone you can't ring everywhere with it.

The second type of VAN is where someone offers a service, say an information database, and charges for

access to it. For example
Euronet-Diane connects up the many
different databases available in
Europe. These networks can have
different levels of access, ranging from
'open' to 'closed'. This is usually
controlled by a password system.

VDU
Visual display unit. Looks like a
television and displays the information
and programmes you're dealing with
in the computer.

Videotext
There are two varieties: Teletext (not
to be confused with teletex) and
viewdata. The first is broadcast via
standard UHF transmission (like
CEEFAX and ORACLE) and the
second is delivered on cables (like
Prestel).

Teletext is a one-way system which
piggybacks digital data on the
television broadcast signal by inserting
its messages in the unused lines of the
vertical interval. The user has a
keyboard the size of a calculator to
select pages. It's not 'interactive' so
you can't ask for more information.

Viewdata is an interactive system
and uses a telephone line or coaxial
cable and is usually accessed using a
modem (see above).

154

The old coaxial cable (left), developed over 50 years ago, measures 4.5 inches and is stuffed with copper cables. It carries fewer conversations than the new lightwave cable (right), which has a set of 12 'ribbons' of glass fibres and measures only half-an-inch across.

Bibliography

United States

Push Button Fantasies: Critical Perspectives on Videotex and Information Technology.
Vincent Mosco. Ablex Publishing Corp., 355 Chesnut Street, Norwood N.J., USA. 1982.

Telematics and Government.
Dan Schiller. Ablex Publishing Corporation. 1982.

Canada

Dependency Road: Communications, Capitalism, Consciousness and Canada.
Dallas Smythe. Ablex Publishing Corporation. 1981.

Europe

Télématique, Mythes et Réalités.
Jean-Claude Quiniou. Edition Gallimard, Paris, 1980.

Japan

The Information Society as Post-Industrial Society.
Yoneji Masuda. Institute for Information Society. Tokyo, 1980.

Third World

Broadcasting in the Third World: Promise and Performance.
Elihu Katz and George Wedell. Macmillan, London, 1978.

Electronic Colonialism: The Future of International Broadcasting and Communication.
Thomas L. McPhail, Sage Publications Ltd., London and Beverly Hills, 1981.

United Kingdom

New Technologies, New Policies?
John Howkins, Broadcasting Research Unit, British Film Institute, London, 1982.

Comedia Publishing Group

9 Poland St, London W1

Comedia Publishing produces books on all aspects of the media including: the press and publishing; TV, radio and film; and the impact of new communications technology.

The Comedia publishing series is based on contemporary research of relevance to media and communications studies courses, though it is also aimed at general readers, activists and specialists in the field.

The series is exceptional because it spans the media from the mainstream and commercial to the oppositional, radical and ephemeral.

No. 13

MICRO-CHIPS WITH EVERYTHING – The consequences of information technology

Edited by Paul Sieghart

Information Technology is the result of the rapid advance of telecommunications and computing technologies. Books on the subject so far have been confined to either specialist areas or the needs of the computer buff; this book recognises that IT affects every aspect of our lives – the political, social and cultural. Alan Benjamin, Clive Jenkins, Mike Cooley, Patricia Hewitt and Stuart Hood.

paperback £3.50 hardback £9.50

Published jointly with the Institute of Contemporary Arts

No. 12

THE WORLD WIRED UP – Unscrambling the new communications puzzle

by Brian Murphy

Will the new computer-communications systems really create the social revolution in work and leisure they promise? This book attempts to puncture the hot air balloon on which the industry currently rides by firstly cutting through the jargon to describe the new systems – especially satellite broadcasting, cable television and 'informatics' – and then explaining how the world market is being carved up by the multi-nationals. Brian Murphy's lucid text sorts out the main players and their products and also examines the options for control available to governments and citizens.

paperback £3.50 hardback £9.50

No. 11

WHAT'S THIS CHANNEL FOUR? – An alternative report

edited by Simon Blanchard and David Morley

Arguments about what sort of service a Fourth TV Channel should provide go back more than 20 years. But now it has finally become reality, alongside its Welsh counterpart. Will Channel 4 live up to the expectations of innovation and experimentation – not simply providing an ITV2? This handbook explains how a major new broadcasting service was created, how it works from the inside, analyses the arguments about what programmes it will produce and shows how viewers can influence the content.

paperback £3.50 hardback £9.50